# THE KITCHEN GARDENER

*How to Recycle Your Leftovers to Grow Fruits and Vegetables Inside Your Home*

## Madeline Dolowich

BEAUFORT BOOKS, INC.
*New York* / *Toronto*

Some material in this book has been quoted from "How to Read a Plant Food Label" and "Don't Throw It, Grow It" from Popular Gardening.

Library of Congress Cataloging in Publication Data

Dolowich, Madeline.
    The kitchen gardener.

    1. Fruit-culture.  2. Vegetable gardening.  3. Indoor gardening.
4. Plant propagation.  I. Title.
SB357.27.D64        635'.0483        81-3826
ISBN 0-8253-0070-3                AACR2

Published in the United States by Beaufort Books, Inc., New York.
Published simultaneously in Canada by Nelson, Foster and Scott Ltd.
Printed in the U.S.A.        First Beaufort Edition

10   9   8   7   6   5   4   3   2   1

# THE
# KITCHEN
# GARDENER

# ACKNOWLEDGMENTS

I would like to thank the Essex County Park Commission's Center for Environmental Studies in Roseland, New Jersey; Eileen Greason, Park Caretaker; Auggie Alviggi, Center Manager; Kate Alfriend of the United States Department of Agriculture; Geo. Park Seed Co., Inc.; and Bob Stark, Special Projects Manager of the Public Service Lamp Corporation.

*I dedicate this book to the memory of
Aunt Sally, Uncle Mac, and Aunt Jeanette.*

# CONTENTS

Introduction      13

**PART 1: THE BASICS      21**
How to Select a Pot      23
About Soil and Watering      30
Nutrition      36
Lighting      45
Pests and Other Plant Ailments      55

**PART 2: FRUITS      63**
Your First Project: The Date      65
Cherries      68
The Mango      71
The Peach      74
The Plum      77
The Persimmon      79
The Guava      81
The Papaya      83
The Apple      86
The Kiwi      89
Grapes      91
The Pomegranate      94
The Prickly Pear      97
The Pineapple      99
The Banana      102
Citrus      105
The Honeydew Melon      108
The Avocado      110
The Coconut      113

**PART 3: NUTS     117**
The Almond     119
The Peanut     121
Sunflowers     124

**PART 4: VEGETABLES     127**
Garlic     129
Beets     131
Lentils     133
Peas     135
The Sweet Potato     138
Lima Beans     141
Turnips     143
Soybeans     145
Garbanzo Beans     147
The Love Apple     149
The Carrot     151
Squash     153
The Radish     156
The Parsnip     159
The Cucumber     162

**PART 5: GREENHOUSES     165**
How About a Greenhouse?     167

**PART 6: GLOSSARY     181**

# THE
# KITCHEN
# GARDENER

# INTRODUCTION

If you think back, gardening from kitchen throw-aways has been around for quite some time. Recall when you, as an elementary student, had watched and taken notes in science class while the teacher grew a plant from a sweet potato as part of an experiment.

And while you are testing your memory, remember your grandmother's friendly house plants that had lent a special charm to her already quaint kitchen. Where did she get them? Plant stores were pretty scarce in comparison to the way they have sprung up today. Besides, with all the scrimping and saving that she had to do in order to keep her family in comforts, she wasn't about to spend it all on plants.

So, where did she get all those beautiful plants? Oh, she might have gotten one or two from other sources, but the others were more or less grown out of her own ingenuity. Being a skillful woman in the art of saving, utilizing, and stretching all she could into useful facilities, she grew most of her plants herself. Grandma didn't know it then, but she was busy paving the way for us "modern folk," for not since the Victory Garden days of World War II has gardening hit such a high in popularity.

The plain truth of the matter is that not only is gardening fun, but it is economical, as well. True, there are plant stores galore, but the bill really adds up if you want to buy more than one or two plants.

Gardening is also a family affair—a project in which

everyone can share. And what better way is there to teach your child about nature?

Kitchen gardening is, in all actuality, a "don't throw it—grow it" method for planting the parts of fruits and vegetables that you would ordinarily toss away. Even nuts and beans are potentials for future decorative foliage. And remember that beautiful plant with the bright purple-veined leaves that Grandma had in her kitchen? That was grown from a beet that she had considered not quite good enough to feed her brood. Yet, she didn't waste it, did she?

Now you can do the same thing. You don't need a green thumb either, because it's easy. Anyone can do it, no matter how unsuccessful a gardener they might have been in the past. You will find that everything in this book has been pretty well mapped out and the instructions are simple.

If you are an individual who loves the presence of greenery, but does not want to have to water every time you turn around, believe it or not there is an answer to this problem. The solution can even be found in the ground-floor basics of choosing a pot. But there are still other ways in which to get around having to water too often.

Using a good, rich soil is something that should not be taken lightly. How many times have you used soil from your backyard to try to maintain plant life? Perhaps you might have had some luck, but chances are that it supplied insufficient properties and the plant couldn't live. If it did, perhaps it was puny and hardly seemed to grow.

Furthermore, the plant may have become infested with insects that sucked and drew the life from the leaves, until finally, its roots and stem withered from the attack and died. Surprisingly, it is not always easy to spot plant pests as many of them are microscopic. As we go along, you'll discover how you can recognize the presence of harmful insects and learn what to do to destroy them. Even if you had floundered around and had achieved success in getting rid of the adults, did you go back later to kill off the young 'uns? Chances are you didn't.

And what about your plant's nutrition? We give ourselves the best of care, take vitamins, and make sure that we eat a well-balanced diet. Well, why shouldn't we do the same thing for our plants?

There are many types of fertilizers out on the market today but poor Grandma couldn't rely on such conveniences in her time. She had to make her own plant food, saving such things as egg shells, coffee grounds, and anything else she could think of to make into compost. As for us, all we have to do is choose which plant food is the most convenient to use. They run the gamut from mixing the concoction yourself to spraying already-prepared formulas directly onto the soil itself.

To some people, choosing the right fertilizer can be a real problem. Learning to understand when to feed a plant and how much to give it is also a crucial matter. Realizing the importance of this particular issue, I have included a chapter dealing with all aspects of plant food.

However, since we, here, are not scientists but laymen whose only interest is in raising and taking proper care of plants, I have approached the subject with simplicity.

Which brings me to another matter. With the plant

thriving on a good diet, such as it is, normal growth
will eventually progress to the point where leaves and
branches advance to a too-dense stage. Therefore, a
thinning out becomes necessary. This is known as
pruning. You might think of pruning much in the same
vein as you would haircuts for people.

Another term, however, with which to become acquainted is pinching back. This is a matter of removing the terminal bud, the bud growing on the very tip
of the branch from where all new growth is coming.
This, like pruning, helps to make a bushier plant and
also allows more room for growing.

In comparing these two methods, pruning is a more
drastic measure to use. Not only does the plant become
more full, but in removing "weak wood" on fruit trees,
for example, the tree is better able to concentrate all of
its growing power on growing better fruit rather than
on extra unwanted branches.

A plant that has a short life cycle, such as the peanut,
will not benefit from such extensive cutting. All you
would get is a short plant. Needless to say, this effect is
not desired. Instead, as with any of the other annuals,
pinching back is more commonly employed.

In this book, you will, as you already know, learn
how to grow fruit trees from the pits of different fruits.
Before we go on, there are a few things you should
know. Potted fruit trees grown inside the house do not,
as a rule, bear fruit. And even if by some chance there
should be fruit, it would be impossible to predict what
kind you would get from what you have planted.

Dr. Miklos Faust, Chief of the Fruit Branch, Agricultural Research Center of the United States Depart-

ment of Agriculture in Washington, D.C., has stated that there is only *one chance* in eighty-thousand that you'll get *exactly* what you have planted. This is because all fruits are hybrids. They are crossed back and forth in order to achieve the desired results.

For example, if you plant a seed from the golden delicious apple, you might get a small apple. On the other hand, you could also wind up with a large apple. The fruit could be white or it could even be red. Although it is not likely that the apple will be the same as the apple from which you took the seed, chances are that you'll still get an edible fruit.

However, the story is quite different with citrus. Very often seeds develop from the ovary without pollination. In this case, the fruit doesn't carry the father's characteristics, only the mother's. Therefore, there is a high probability that you would get the same kind of fruit from where the seeds came.

Once you get your plants growing, you must decide where they can be kept in the house. Generally speaking, most house plants adapt very well to the climactic conditions of your home. Still, despite their tolerance, they can only withstand just so much.

Although not that much know-how is needed, the extra bit of knowledge that you could put to use would certainly go a long, long way. Help your plants to survive the warmer months by protecting them from brutally hot summer days. And give them equal attendance over the cold season. Protect them from drafts and frosty window panes.

Basically, there is only one main ingredient necessary for gardening and that is common sense. Upon growing things from scratch it seems to triple and quadruple so that you, in time, acquire a certain in-tuneness with the plant. You will eventually and ultimately learn to respond to the plant's needs, and it, in turn, can have no choice but to flourish under your tender but confident ministrations. Even if you are a new gardener, prepare to amaze yourself with the dexterity that you can't help but develop.

Sometimes, though, even the best of conditions can result in a failure or two. More, perhaps. Should this happen, do not despair. As I have said, this can happen to anyone and need not have any bearing on your prowess as a gardener. Simply breathe a sigh and chalk it up to an unfortunate incident.

And what have you got to lose? It isn't as if you had lost a great investment in expensive store-bought plants. That is part of the beauty connected with gardening with garbage. You have to purchase groceries anyway, right? Apple seeds are always plentiful as are peanuts and such. Just start the project over. Success is sure to win out. When it does, rest assured, you will feel very proud of yourself, indeed.

Let's see now, what is in that bag of groceries you have just bought. Oranges with which to squeeze fresh juice for the family, a pineapple, because company is expected, unprocessed sunflower seeds that you intend to put out, sweet potatoes for the casserole you want to serve with the baked chicken, and—oh, is that a box of lentils for the soup you're going to make?

And what's that? Fresh beets with which to make a tasty marinated relish? Why, you have the potentials for a whole bunch of house plants already.

Except for the purchase of a good potting mixture and some attractive flower pots, the price is just right. Next to nothing. Yet, there is everything to gain. You couldn't find a better bargain anywhere.

Garbage gardening offers such a wide variety of possibilities that even when you finish reading this book you will constantly be alert for new things to try and grow. Once your appetite has been piqued, there'll be no stopping you.

Remember how only the other week your friend amazed you with the avocado plant she grew from the pit of the fruit? Well, just think how good you'll feel when you show her the plant you grew from the seeds of the papaya.

And don't be too surprised when "it" catches on. Your friends will come to you wanting to know how in the world you did it, so they can do it too.

By then, you'll have become a real pro and will be able to explain it very matter-of-factly. Give yourself a pat on the back then, because you'll have earned it.

Before we begin, there's one more important point to discuss, one that is usually missing from most gardening reading material, and that is the matter of patience. It should be clearly understood that gardening is not something that can be hurried along to meet one's requirements. Nature *must* take Her course.

Understandably, some things take longer to germinate than others, such as the date pit. And so does the peach pit with its hard outer covering.

If you feel impatient and wish to see quick results as encouragement for your efforts, try planting the seeds of any one of the citrus fruits first. However, even they require a certain amount of time before the first shoot can poke its way up through the soil.

There are people who plant something on one day and become disappointed if they do not see results by the following week. Mistakenly, they reach the conclusion that the project has failed and, discouraged, throw it away. Had they been patient and seen their endeavors through, their waiting would have paid off.

That's one thing about people. They are wonderfully curious creatures and will try to do practically anything even though they don't know the correct procedure.

Let me point out again that there will be no need for hit or miss methods here, as all the guesswork has been completely eliminated for your convenience. Therefore, I know of no reason why anyone at all cannot become successful in growing live, healthy plants when they are shown how.

So why don't we get started now. Get out that fresh produce again. Let's see, there are those apples, oh, yes, the oranges, and then there's the. . . .

# PART 1: THE BASICS

# HOW TO SELECT A POT

Although there are certain things to know about pots, choosing the container that you want, in the end, is strictly up to you. What one person may advocate might not be to your liking and vice versa. The truth of the matter is, no matter which pot you use, if you do not take care of your plants—water them, feed them regularly—none of the containers you use can save them.

On the other hand, if you grow your plants in any kind of a container, no matter what it is, even if it is an empty vessel of exquisite beauty that at one time might have held delicate cakes or pretty spools of thread, if you take proper care of your plants, they will survive in almost anything.

However, there are still certain basic facts to discuss pertaining to the different characteristics of flower pots out on the market today. They are as follows:

## UNGLAZED CLAY

Unglazed clay has extremely porous qualities. It promotes rapid evaporation, and if you are the type of individual who doesn't like to be a slave to the watering procedure, then take these facts into consideration.

Because water *does* evaporate so quickly with unglazed clay, the need to water your plants more often is greatly increased. You might be surprised to find during the day, that even though you watered early in the morning, the soil in the pot has already become pretty dry. Check your plant daily for water needs and do not

(23

permit too many days to go by without watering again.

Another characteristic of unglazed clay is that it maintains the desired cool temperature. This is much to the liking of the plant's roots. If, by some chance, the container was left sitting on top of a window sill that has been warming up to a great degree from the direct rays of the sun, unglazed clay would then be very protective.

These pots come equipped with drainage holes. Not all containers do.

Some people like the terra-cotta color of unglazed clay and incorporate it into the decor of the house. After a while, these pots take on what is referred to as a weather-beaten look, and this type of beauty is, of course, in the eye of the beholder.

When using a brand-new unglazed flower pot for the first time, you must break it in. This is accomplished by dunking it in hot water which acts as a preconditioner to the clay material. After all bubbling has ceased, remove the vessel from the water.

This preconditioning prevents the loss of precious moisture from the soil after it has been placed in the pot. For this reason, it is not practical to skip the procedure. If you do, the plant will not be getting a sufficient amount of water, even if you are properly watering it every time. This is because the porosity of the clay is absorbing part of the moisture.

In addition, it is also necessary to place a piece of broken pottery over the drainage hole. The purpose of this is to prohibit soil from seeping through the opening every time you water the plant, while still allowing for proper drainage.

## CERAMIC

Ceramic is not as porous as unglazed clay. While it is still necessary to water frequently, it does not require the same urgency as the above mentioned.

Because ceramic flower pots do not come equipped with drainage holes, you must mend the situation yourself. Before you place a plant in this type of container you must place a piece of shard, broken pottery, or pebbles at the bottom.

Despite the fact that ceramic is not as protective a substance as unglazed clay, it still has qualities protective enough to insulate the plant's roots against a too warm environment.

When watering, be careful about overdoing it. You don't want to create a waterlogged condition. Excess moisture could cause the roots of the plant to rot and in the end, the plant will die. Remember, there are no drainage holes, only the drainage you've supplied.

## PLASTIC

Plastic pots are not as breakable as containers made from other substances. Nor do they cost as much. They come in a large assortment of sizes and some even come equipped with their own saucers.

Plastic is light and thin. It is quite popular on the plant scene today. There are a few basic colors from which you can choose. In addition, they are equipped with drainage holes that are so necessary for proper plant maintenance. When you buy the pot, check the bottom to make sure that the drainage holes are not closed. If closed, open by punching them out with a sharp implement.

Because plastic is not a porous fabric, plants do not have to be watered so frequently. This is a point that should be considered if you do not like the task of watering on a daily basis. You can go twice as long without having to water as you would with unglazed clay.

However, plastic is not as good an insulator as unglazed clay. The plant's roots are less protected from the direct rays of the sun when living thusly. Watch for overly warm situations so that overheating doesn't result.

## GLASS

The characteristics of glass are pretty similar to plastic. If it is transparent, you might possibly find green or brown algae growing between the glass and the moist soil.

Because glass is not porous, do not water too often or the soil and the plant's delicate roots will become waterlogged. Again, here the roots could rot and the plant could die. To play it safe, always keep a watchful eye on the plant. Water just enough to moisten when soil becomes dry.

To allow for proper drainage, place a layer of gravel or a broken piece of pottery at the bottom of the vessel. However, even with these precautionary measures, guard against overwatering when using glass as a container.

As you may already know, glass heats up quickly, thus the need to provide a safe atmosphere for the plant. A glass flower pot left sitting on top of a window sill that is heating up from the direct rays of the sun is bound to become too hot. Again, excessive heat can burn and destroy sensitive roots, thereby resulting in complete loss of the plant.

## WOOD

The characteristics of wood are thick and *somewhat* porous. In fact, its qualities are pretty similar to plastic, decreasing the necessity of having to water too often.

Wooden containers come in a variety of shapes and sizes such as rectangular or square boxes, tubs, hanging slatted baskets, and half barrels, which were, at one time, used to age wine and whiskey.

Kiln-dried redwood is usually used, although cedar is almost as popular. Both woods contribute to the beauty of any decor. They can resist damage from termites and each weathers well.

You will find that not only are wooden containers popular, but they are relatively inexpensive as well. However, they contain no drainage holes. Therefore, proper drainage must be supplied by providing a layer of gravel or a broken piece of pottery at the bottom of the vessel.

Some wooden containers are more apt to deteriorate than others. Those that have been reinforced with metal bands are more sturdy than ones that are held together with nails or glue.

Half barrels as well as tubs also become quite heavy after filling with soil. Furthermore, they weigh heavily after a plant has been watered.

## PAPER

A recent innovation in flower pots can be found in pressed paper. They are available in many sizes and are inexpensive.

Pressed paper pots are lightweight. However, weight can be a disadvantage here because if the container is left outside on the patio or porch and there is a fairly strong wind brewing, it can be knocked over.

Another disadvantage lies in the fact that if a plant becomes top-heavy, it can be a strain to the lightweight pressed paper pot. Its light weight is unable to support the condition of the plant and it can fall over easily.

## REPOTTING

Whichever pot you use, make sure that the plant inside does not become pot-bound. Here are some guidelines that you can follow.

> REPOT WHEN:
> a plant appears to be scrawny
> it has stopped growing entirely
> you can see roots coming through the drainage holes
>
> BEWARE: In case you keep more than one plant in a single container, watch that they do not begin to crowd each other. Should this occur, repot immediately or strangulation can result.

To remove a plant from its old pot, place your fingers around the stem to hold the soil in place. Then invert the plant and tap the edge of the container. The plant, together with the ball of soil, should come sliding into your hand.

Do not disturb the old soil you see adhering to the roots.

In transplanting, use the next size up to increase pot diameter and depth by one or two inches. Before using, douse the container with hot water to help ward off fungus.

Place the plant in the pot and fill in the space under and around the roots with a good potting mixture. Take care not to pack it down too tightly. When you finish, the soil level should be about an inch below the rim. Tap the container to help settle the soil, then water lightly.

# ABOUT SOIL AND WATERING

Now that we've discussed containers, let's talk about what kind of soil to use inside of them. We've already established that using soil from the backyard is not feasible.

If you want to produce a healthy plant, you cannot use poor soil. Perhaps the plant will be able to survive this way, but at its best, it will be a scrawny weakling.

The basic structure of lesser quality soil is extremely fine. After a time, it hardens like cement, thus encapsulating the plant in a tomb. There, no precious air or water can penetrate to tender roots.

Keeping these facts in mind, always begin with a good potting soil mixture. It should consist roughly of about forty percent air space so that the plant's roots can have freedom to grow and breathe easily. Good soil should have a loose consistency and fall apart when you rub it between your fingers.

Because you want to use good soil, there are a couple of things you can do. One is to buy a sterile, well-balanced composition. The other is to mix your own.

Unless directions state otherwise when dealing with a particular plant, the Essex County Park Commission's Center for Environmental Studies in Roseland, New Jersey, recommends a recipe containing one part garden loam, one part builder's sand, and one part peat moss or leaf mold.

Garden loam is a rich soil that is made up of clay,

sand, and organic matter. Builder's sand is coarse and helps to aerate heavy soil. Peat moss and leaf mold are both organic materials which improve upon the soil's water-holding ability.

Other things you will come in contact with are vermiculite and sphagnum moss. It helps it to retain moisture and the necessary nutrients so important for a plant's good health.

Sphagnum moss grows in very wet areas. It looks like a bird's nest, if you've ever seen it as a backing for the Staghorn Fern. Sphagnum moss is also used as a soil conditioner and for a medium in which to germinate seeds.

When making your own potting soil mixture, there is always the possibility that insect eggs and larvae could be present. For this reason, the mixture must be sterilized.

Therefore, put the moist composition into the oven. Then bake it at two-hundred degrees for not less than forty-five minutes. Make sure that the mixture has completely cooled before using it on your plants.

When this has been completed, place the soil in a plastic bag. Fasten it securely, locking in the moisture. Soil, understand, should always be kept moist, never soggy or overly dry.

Which brings to mind the matter of watering. Plants, as a rule, absorb water through their roots. That is why, when a watering schedule is being maintained, you should always water your plants thoroughly each time.

If you water little and often, the surface of the soil is merely dampened. Roots cannot get sufficient moisture this way and can dry up and die as a result.

Stating a definite law about when to water would not be prudent because how much you should water depends largely upon the environmental status of your home. For example, if the atmosphere is more to the dry side, then plants will require frequent watering. Naturally, if the humidity in your home is high, then the need to water too often is somewhat decreased.

Notice, when you water, how much heavier the plant's container feels. Notice, too, that the soil takes on a much darker color. When you touch the soil, it feels moist.

As the soil begins to dry, see how the surface becomes much lighter in color. It has a dry and sandy feel when touched. When it feels that way—water!

Here are some watering aids to consider.

## THE SELF-WATERER

What can an individual do when he loves his plants but simply abhors the chore of the watering routine? He doesn't mean to let the plant dry out, but somehow the days go by and before you know it, wilting has occured.

And what can a person do when there are no neighbors around to take care of your plants when you are going away for a two-week vacation? Who will see that it gets all the water it needs?

Why, the self-waterer, of course!

With this automatic watering mechanism, a gimmick is devised which can be inserted into the soil of the plant's container. Then water is dispensed from a wick which is part of the reservoir set-up containing a particular amount of water.

The size of the reservoir determines just how much water can be used. For example, you might use a reservoir that can hold as much as two gallons of water.

Water is dispensed continuously at the right pace. Your plant will never even know you are away. Upon your return, just fill up the reservoir again, and you're all set for another two weeks. Your plant will be sufficiently watered while you simply watch and enjoy.

## THE PEBBLE TRAY

This is another way in which you can make the watering routine an easier task. Although this method is relatively simple, it is quite effective, an ideal way to water many plants all at the same time.

Purchase a pebble tray at your local plant store. Then load it with pebbles and fill it up with water. Not so much that it overflows, but just enough to cover the pebbles.

Place a number of plants on top of this set-up. Each plant will receive all the moisture it requires by drawing it in through the bottom of its container.

In order for plants to continue drawing water in this fashion, never allow the water in the tray to completely evaporate. Always maintain the same water level and you'll have no trouble.

Keep this up and your plants can continue to survive in this manner indefinitely.

## A POT WITHIN A POT

This is a good method to use with unglazed pots. All you have to do is line a large container with drenched sphagnum moss. Then place a smaller container inside. If you continue to keep the sphagnum moss good and wet, moisture, somehow, will seep its way into the inner pot.

If this method sounds simple, that's because it is. And it works, too!

## THE MOISTURE METER

Any assistance with watering problems is always welcome. The moisture meter is just one more device on which you can rely. It works on a very simple principle.

What this is really, is a thermometer type of affair that is placed directly into the soil. Outside, a dial indicates exactly how much moisture is present.

If the needle points to a drying condition, then it is time to water. Otherwise, conditions, according to how much moisture a particular plant needs, are perfect.

In effect, the moisture meter *is* like reading a thermometer. Because it is so easy to use, perhaps this handy gadget is for you.

## THE PLASTIC BAG

This is an *excellent* method of watering your plants while you are away on vacation. No matter how long you are gone! Use this method all year 'round if you wish.

Simply water each of your plants well. Enclose them individually in medium to large-sized plastic bags. Fasten securely. For standing plants, use the oversized plastic bag that the tailor puts over cleaned and pressed garments.

What you are creating here is, in effect, a terrarium. Soon after you have placed the plastic over your plants, notice the dew that is already forming all over the inside of the bags.

# NUTRITION

Plants, as do all other living things, need a well-balanced diet so that they may grow strong and healthy. To achieve such a healthful status, they require at least sixteen different basic nutrients, each one vital in its own way. Divided into three groups, they are the major elements, commonly referred to as N-P-K, which consist of nitrogen, phosphorous, and potassium.

Nitrogen, an odorless, transparent gas, is imperative for cell reproduction, therefore constituting the sustainment of all forms of life.

## THE DIFFERENT PLANT FOODS

What exactly is fertilizer? In answer, it can best be described as any material that supplies nutrients required for the growth and development of plants. Natural or organic fertilizers, classified as water insolubles, consist of elements that have been derived from living matter containing carbon.

Prime examples of these organic compounds include bone meal, sewerage sludge, blood, kitchen compost, and manure teas which are made by putting manure into a burlap bag, then dunking it in water like a tea bag.

As micro-organisms in the soil break down these compounds, organic nitrogen becomes available to the plant. Because of its low nutrient analysis, organics take large quantities to supply an efficient rate of nitrogen. And due to its slow release, initial response can be delayed for many days in soil that is too cool.

Inorganic plant food is a nitrogen source found naturally or is synthesized from organic compounds such as ammonium sulfate, calcium nitrate, and ammonium phosphate. In direct contrast to the natural type of foods, they do not contain carbon.

This form of nitrogen makes itself readily available to the plant. When dissolved in water, roots are quick to absorb it. This can come in handy when there is the need to supply nutrient salts to a deficient plant in a hurry. However, because of its fast release ability, its lingering effectiveness is minimal, so frequent applications of this water soluble food may be necessary.

Other examples of inorganic fertilizers are ammonium nitrate, potassium nitrate, and potassium chloride. Because water soluble fertilizers are so readily available for absorption, they are best suited for house plants.

Pertaining to synthetic organics, this nitrogen source is synthesized by using carbon containing ammonia and carbon dioxide. Urea, the first synthetic organic to be developed, is similar to inorganics in that they, too, are water soluble. Some manufacturers have found a way in which to combine urea and formaldehyde, but with no quality control manufacturing, the product would have no predictable release rate. Furthermore, the quality of this product is akin to plastic plates. But only a small amount of this has leaked into the plant food industry.

Actually, the only "free" elements that plants probably receive are hydrogen, oxygen, and carbon, which are obtained from air and water. But without proper watering, correct soil, and the plain common sense care that plants need, no fertilizer in the world could possibly live up to its expectations.

Today, there are many different kinds of plant foods to choose from. Liquid fish emulsion, for example, is among them. Using this kind of plant food is akin to giving a plant a good dose of cod liver oil. Long ago Indians used to bury fish heads in the soil to enrich their crops.

A new product on the market is an odorless organic food in the form of a spike. It is pre-measured, easy to use, and will not burn the plant. To use it, the spike is pushed into the soil around the plant half-way between the stem and the pot until it has almost disappeared below the surface. There, it dispenses the correct amounts of food at proper intervals.

Concentrated liquids diluted in water begin to work immediately, but because the concentration of active ingredients differ with individual brands, it is important to follow the manufacturer's instructions. And in this book, unless specific instructions are given about a particular project, please, by all means, *DO* as the formulator says.

Time release pellets, coated products, promise slow release. They release their nutrients when they come in contact with water. Nutrients are drawn through the wall of the pellets, where designated amounts of nitrogen, phosphorous, and potassium are metered out to the roots of the plant.

However, their coating can be harmed by physical damage and by temperature. This can affect the fast release of the soluble N-P-K. In addition, excess water can release these elements too quickly. These pellets are termed "hot" nitrogen. In salt form, they can promote "salt" build-up and burn the plant.

Among the fertilizers of today are granular combinations which are pressed into tablets. They, too, contain this "hot" nitrogen as does a pill that nurseries put out.

While it is true that most consumer products have been of the "hot" nitrogen type, historically speaking, it was the only kind of plant food available. The advantage here, though, is that it provides instant food. It should, however, be doled out in small quantities. And often.

Another new plant food that has come out on the market is a fertilizer that can be sprayed directly onto the soil itself. This can be particularly useful to the "non-green thumbist" in that it eliminates guesswork completely and there is no mess. A few measured squirts about every three or four weeks and the plant absorbs its readily available nutrients on contact.

## HOW TO READ A PLANT FOOD LABEL

Just as it is important to know how to read the label on a bottle of vitamins prepared for human consump-

tion, so is it essential to be able to comprehend the contents that make up the plant food label. Using the House in Bloom plant food label as an example, we turn again to the major elements, or N-P-K, as previously mentioned. It is they that constitute the fertilizer analysis.

Always in this order, they are nitrogen, phosphorous, and potassium. Their available amounts are depicted by fertilizer ratio, the series of numbers shown at the top of all plant food labels.

Although the House in Bloom foliage plant ratio we are using for an example reads 7-7-7, the order of things would remain the same, even if the ratio were to read 5-10-5. For example, 5-10-5 would designate that 5% nitrogen was present in the formula, 10% phosphoric acid, and 5% potassium.

However, in keeping with the 7-7-7 ratio, imagine that there are one-hundred pounds of fertilizer. Out of this amount, the fertilizer will contain seven percent or seven pounds of nitrogen, seven percent or seven pounds of phosphorous, and seven percent or seven pounds of potassium. This means that out of the one-hundred pounds of fertilizer, there are twenty-one pounds of these nutrients present.

Listed first on the label are the elements that go into making up the seven percent of total nitrogen. Since nitrogen is the main source of foliage growth, it can make all the difference between really good growth to fair to stunted. It is also responsible for the intensity of green color.

The 2.6% urea nitrogen which is shown next, is a water soluble substance that is a very good source of nitrogen. It is derived from the chemical urea.

We then skip down to the 2.3% of ammoniacal nitrogen. This is a substance that resembles ammonia. Before this material and the above mentioned urea can be turned into nitrate nitrogen, which is listed here in the amount of 2.1%, they must first undergo certain changes brought about by moisture, heat, and microorganisms present in the soil. When these changes are completed, it is then readily absorbed by the roots of the plant.

In adding up the 2.6% urea nitrogen, the 2.3% of ammoniacal nitrogen, and the 2.1% of nitrate nitrogen, you will see that they add up to seven percent of total nitrogen.

Next we have available phosphoric acid, 7%. It is chemically known as $P_2O_5$, and is always the second number on the plant food ratio. Phosphorous, mined in the form of phosphate rock, is the element that is responsible for developing roots and aids in the flowering of flowering plants. Like iron, it can combine with other elements in the soil and become unavailable to the plant. However, chelating it will permit the plant to continue absorbing it through its roots.

Further on down the label, we come to the listing that designates the presence of soluble potash, 7%. Potassium chloride and potassium sulfate are two common sources. The chemical symbol for potash is $K_2O$. Potash is a raw material that is mined. It helps the plant to resist disease and aids in the formation of starches and sugars needed for strong roots. In addition, it acts as a balancing agent between nitrogen and phosphorous as well as on other essential ones. Without it, leaves would become white around their edges. They would look burned or scorched.

To continue, the statement regarding primary plant nutrients is next. In reality, it is self-explanatory in that it simply tells where all the nutrients that have been listed on the label come from.

They are derived from ammonium phosphate, potassium nitrate, and urea. These are water soluble ingredients that have been incorporated into the formulation of the product.

Upon reaching the bottom of the plant food label there is the expression: "potential acidity equal to 235 lbs. of calcium carbonate $CaCo_3$ per ton."

Potential acidity is a measure of the acid-forming potential of a fertilizer. The figure here is listed in pounds of calcium carbonate needed to neutralize one ton of fertilizer. Manufacturers give this information because different plants require different acid levels. For example, acid-loving plants thrive in soils that have low pH. This term specifies the amount of acid that is present in the soil. The higher the pH, the less acid present. The lower the pH, the more acid is present. Therefore, when speaking about potential acidity, we talk of the potential of chemical fertilizers to form acids in the soil. Hence, calcium carbonate is used as a standard measure per ton, or for so many pounds.

As you will notice, the net weight stated on the plant food label is eight ounces. Because manufacturers must adhere to the strict standards that have been set up by both State and Federal government agencies, the consumer is guaranteed that he will indeed receive the full amount promised.

A particular point of interest lies in the fact that

manufacturers have taken into account the tendency for people to overfeed a plant and have taken precautionary measures to that effect. But the rule still stands, that no matter which type of fertilizer the consumer selects, it is very important to carefully follow the instructions of that individual manufacturer.

Unless a plant is growing under artificial light, omit feeding it during its dormant period, November through March. Plants need their time to rest and slow down in their growing.

Neither should a plant with dry soil be fed. It needs moisture first. Such a plant has extremely sensitive roots and giving it food will only burn them.

In repotting, wait between two to four weeks before fertilizing so the roots of the plant can resume growing and absorb the food. In other words, the plant needs time in which to adapt to its new surroundings.

Actually, the overall appearance of a plant can speak for itself. If a plant looks healthy enough, it might not even require food. And unless it is being visibly attacked by insects, fertilizer might be the very thing to bolster up a faded-looking specimen. So, as you can see, there really is no set rule when to fertilize a plant.

## TROUBLESHOOTING

Mishandling plant food can have harmful side-effects on your plants. A prime example of this can be found in severe overfeeding and underwatering, particularly with foliage plants.

What will happen is that they will grow at too rapid a pace, causing weakness and wilting. Furthermore, there is the danger of "salt" build-up from too much fertilizer. White crust invades the soil and settles on the rim of the pot.

To remedy this, the plant should be given more light. Feeding it less often, using half the usual dosage of food also helps. Then, the salt that has accumulated must be leached out of the plant by flushing it repeatedly with water.

Provision should be made for the plant to drain into a sink or some other receptacle. Otherwise, if the plant is allowed to remain sitting in its watery saucer, it will only suck up the "salt" again while it dries.

Overfeeding flowering plants has its problems, too. This is true when plant food especially high in nitrogen content has been used. What happens here is that there will be an abundance of foliage, but at the expense of the flowers. In addition, green scum can cling to the pot.

To remedy this, the plant should be fed less often with half the usual amount of food. The green scum should be washed off. In the case of underfeeding, the plant's lower leaves lose their color and they fall off. Feeding it during its growing period helps.

In fertilizing foliage plants, a fertilizer ratio of 2-2-2 or similar should be used. For flowering plants, 1-2-1 or similar.

But the best thing to do to insure the well-being of your plants is to *always* follow the manufacturer's instructions.

# LIGHTING

There's no getting away from the fact that light is essential to plants. It assists leaves in converting carbon dioxide and water into sugar and starch, the plant's basic foods. Eventually, it will combine them with elements from the soil and manufacture all the materials required for good growth.

Plants need all the colors that go into making up sunlight, but in the proper proportions. Blue and red rays effect plant growth the greatest. Supplied in just the right amounts, they aid the plant in creating large quantities of starch. When it is dark, this stored nutrition is drawn upon as a source of energy.

Getting down to brass tacks, everybody talks about lighting and plants and what do they come up with? Different opinions. Experts try to capture the sun in a flask and then every pro and hobbyist, alike, come running to see if the perfect product has been produced.

The truth of the matter is that nothing can replace natural sunlight, but when it isn't available, artificial lighting is the next best thing. If you talk to a lighting expert, he'll be glad to give you his opinion. Ask another, and he'll be just as glad to give you his. The only thing a person can do is window shop, read all the promises that each manufacturer makes, and then make up your own mind about which lamp to buy.

There are different kinds of lights used for various purposes. For example, high pressure sodium is an efficient artificial light source as far as illumination is concerned. These are the yellow lights you see being used as street or security lighting. Because of its bulkiness and heaviness, it is difficult for the layman to use in the home or office. A four-hundred watt unit weighs about fifty-three pounds. This type of light is unsuitable for indoor plants.

Metal halide is a light source usually found lighting up night-games at the ball park. It is highly unstable because the light discolors. In addition, it has a relatively short life span for a high intensity lamp. This is sporadically found in public areas supplying light for plants. It is not recommended for home or office use.

Mercury vapor is another source of artificial lighting. It has been successfully used for growing and maintaining foliage plants in public areas, but it is not recommended for home or office use.

The fluorescent tube is highest on the scale of efficiency, but lowest on the scale of projection of light. It is still a problem because its bulk makes it difficult for the architect and designer to place them decoratively in home and office environments.

There are some fluorescent lamps, however, that are high enough in red and blue rays to start seedlings of flowers and vegetables until they are ready to be transplanted outdoors. The cool white fluorescent tube was the first one used for such purposes.

Later, Gro-Lux tubes were developed expressly for growing plants to take them right up to the stage prior to outdoor planting. However, the tubes mentioned thus far didn't produce far enough red wavelengths of light imperative for flowering.

Because the Geo. W. Park Seed Co., Inc. was aware that incandescent bulbs produced the necessary far red wavelengths of light, they came up with the Bloom Lamp which incorporates fluorescent tubes and incandescent bulbs to be used on flowering indoor plants.

The Westinghouse Fluorescent and Vapor Lamp Division introduced Agro-Lite, a fluorescent tube that produces the blue, red, and far red wavelengths of light so necessary for plant life. It is suitable for indoor use.

The self-ballasted mercury vapor works on an incandescent system without the need of special wiring or remote ballast. Wonderlite of the Public Service Lamp Corporation has come a long way with this type of lighting in that it doesn't have to be confined to a shelf but may be used anywhere in the house, particularly in those hard-to-light areas. Furthermore, its balanced spectrum also can double as a display light that will not clash with normal household or office lighting.

Here is a chart I've prepared depicting the different ways that plants respond to various lamps.

## LAMP AND PLANT RESPONSE

| Lamp | Plant Response |
| --- | --- |
| Fluorescent-Cool White (CW) and Warm White (WW). | * Green foliage expands parallel to the surface of the lamp<br>* Stems elongate slowly<br>* Multiple side shoots develop<br>* Flowering occurs over a long period of time |
| Fluorescent-Gro-Lux (GL) and Plant Lights (PL) | * Deep-green foliage which expands, often larger than on plants grown under CW or WW. |

# LAMP AND PLANT RESPONSE (cont.)

| Lamp | Plant Response |
|------|----------------|
| | * Stem elongates very slowly, extra thick stems develop<br>* Multiple side shoots develop<br>* Flowering occurs late, flower stalk does not elongate |
| Fluorescent-Gro-Lux-WS (GL-WS), Vita-lite (VITA), Agro-lite (AGRO) and Wide Spectrum lamps. | * Light-green foliage which tends to ascend toward the lamp<br>* Stems elongate rapidly, distances between the leaves<br>* Suppresses development of multiple side shoots<br>* Flowering occurs soon, flower stalks elongated, plants mature and age rapidly |
| High Intensity Discharge-Deluxe Mercury (HG) or Metal halide (MH) | * Similar to CW and WW fluorescent lamps compared on equal energy<br>* Green foliage which expands<br>* Stems elongate slowly<br>* Multiple side shoots develop<br>* Flowering occurs over a long period of time |
| High Intensity Discharge-High pressure sodium (HPS) | * Similar to Gro Lux and other color improved fluorescent compared on equal energy<br>* Deep-green foliage which expands, often larger than on plants grown under H and MH<br>* Stems elongate very slowly, extra thick stems develop<br>* Multiple side shoots develop<br>* Flowering occurs late, flower stalks do not elongate |
| High Intensity Discharge-Low Pressure Sodium (LPS) | * Extra deep-green foliage, bigger and thicker than on plants grown under other light sources<br>* Stem elongation is slowed, very thick stems develop |

## LAMP AND PLANT RESPONSE (cont.)

| Lamp | Plant Response |
|---|---|
| | * Multiple side shoots develop even on secondary shoots<br>* Flowering occurs, flower stalks do not elongate |
| | Exceptions: Saintpaulias, lettuce, and Impatiens must have supplemental sunlight or incandescent to insure development of chlorophyll and reduction of stem elongation |
| Incandescent (INC) and Incandescent-Mercury (INC-HG) | * Paling of foliage, thinner and longer than on plants grown under light sources.<br>* Stem elongation is excessive, eventually become spindly and easily breaks<br>* Side shoot development is suppressed, plants expand only in height<br>* Flowering occurs rapidly, the plants mature and senescence takes place |
| | Exceptions: Rosette and thick-leaved plants such as Sansevieria may maintain themselves for many months. The new leaves which eventually develop will elongate and will not have the typical characteristics of the species. |

It is important to use equal energy when converting from one light source to another. Living spaces are lit with natural available light and with many different kinds of lamps. Fluorescent and incandescent lamps are the types most frequently used. Each lamp has a

## RELATIVE LIGHT AND VISIBLE RADIATION OUTPUT OF 40-WATT LAMPS

| 40-Watt Lamp Type Fluorescent | Percent Lumens | Percent Visible Radiation |
|---|---|---|
| Cool White | 100 | 100 |
| Warm White | 100 | 100 |
| Plant Growth | 32 to 60 | 70 to 80 |
| Wide Spectrum - Color Rendering Index (CR1) 90 or above | 60 to 70 | 75 to 85 |

different visible spectrum. To convert from one lamp source to another, use the table "Appropriate Foot-Candles for Equal Radiant Energy."

The foot-candle readings given in this guide are based on Cool White fluorescent lamps. Notice that when the table lists 100 fc of Cool White fluorescent, it requires 53 fc from sunlight, 105 fc from Warm White, 47 fc from Gro-Lux, 68 fc from Gro-Lux-WS to give equal energy and equal effectiveness for lighting plants. Check with a lighting engineer to find out what kind of artificial lamps are used to light the space.

Standard fluorescent lighting fixtures are most easily utilized. Electrical connections require a three-prong plug for safety and positive operation of the lamps. Ungrounded fixtures or lamps without grounded metal reflectors may not operate reliably. Especially noisy fixtures may require ballast replacement.

Components, available at electrical supply stores, can be wired when standard fixtures are not convenient. Always have qualified people install the wiring

## APPROPRIATE FOOT-CANDLES FOR
## EQUAL RADIANT ENERGY

| Lamp | | fc | fc | fc | fc |
|------|------|----|----|----|----|
| **FLUORESCENT** | | | | | |
| Cool White | CW | 100 | 200 | 500 | 1000 |
| Warm White | WW | 105 | 210 | 525 | 1050 |
| Gro-Lux, Plant Light | GRO | 47 | 94 | 235 | 470 |
| Gro-Lux-WS | GRO/WS | 68 | 136 | 340 | 680 |
| Agro-lite | AGRO | 74 | 148 | 370 | 740 |
| Vita-lite | VITA | 80 | 160 | 400 | 800 |
| **DISCHARGE** | | | | | |
| Mercury (all types) | HG | 108 | 216 | 540 | 1080 |
| Metal Halide | MH | 87 | 174 | 435 | 870 |
| High-Pressure Sodium | HPS | 88 | 176 | 440 | 880 |
| Low-Pressure Sodium | LPS | 137 | 274 | 685 | 1370 |
| Incandescent | INC | 35 | 70 | 175 | 350 |
| Incandescent-Mercury | INC-HG | 50 | 100 | 250 | 500 |
| **SUNLIGHT** | | | | | |
| Winter | | 53 | 106 | 265 | 530 |
| Summer | | 55 | 110 | 273 | 546 |

and make sure the wiring meets the local and National Electrical Code. The components necessary are as follows:

**Lampholders** Two are required for each lamp. (U-tubes require special lampholders available at electrical supply stores.)

**Ballast** This is a built-in power regulator.

**Wire** Insulated, heat-resistant type.

**Metal enclosure** This will house the ballast and the wiring to the lampholders.

Plants need light for eight to twelve hours a day. Use an automatic timer to control the length of illumination. Do not depend on your memory to turn on the lamps at the proper time.

An automatic timer is available at hardware and electrical stores. The timer can be set to turn the lamps on and off at anytime. For sixteen hours of light, you can set it to turn on at six o'clock in the morning and off at ten o'clock at night.

Light level determines the types of plants that can be grown. Recommended light levels for plants are given in foot-candles (fc) as you already know. A foot-candle, by the way, is a unit of illumination equal to the amount of light thrown by one standard candle on a surface one foot away.

Plants will grow in higher light levels but they can't survive below the minimum levels of light. For example, with sunlight, low designates a minimum light level of twelve foot-candles and a preferred level of thirty-five to one hundred foot-candles.

Medium designates a minimum of thirty-five foot-candles and a preferred level of one hundred foot-candles while very high designates a minimum of five hundred foot-candles and a preferred level of two hundred fifty foot-candles.

Very high designates a minimum of five hundred foot-candles and a preferred level of over five hundred foot-candles.

Using artificial light with cool white flourescent lamps as the standard, low designates a minimum light level of twenty-five foot-candles and a preferred level of seventy-five to one hundred foot-candles.

Medium designates a minimum of seventy-five to one hundred foot-candles and a preferred level of two hundred to five hundred foot-candles. High designates a minimum of two hundred foot-candles and a preferred level of five hundred foot-candles.

Very high designates a minimum of one thousand foot-candles and a preferred level of over one thousand foot candles.

If the natural light in the living space is insufficient to maintain plants, then artificial light must be used. To determine if adequate light exists, it is necessary to use a light meter. Models, typically, range from ten to fifty foot-candles, fifty to two hundred fifty foot-candles, and two hundred to one thousand foot-candles with an X–10 multiplying cover.

These meters work by positioning their tops parallel to the surface you want to measure for light. The switch position is shifted from high to medium to low to determine the intensity of light being measured in foot-candles. Several readings should be taken so that the results can be averaged to determine the proper light measurement.

In case you are thinking of using a photographic light meter, don't! It is not satisfactory for measuring plant lighting because conversions and corrections are complex due to special variations with different meters.

It is best to purchase a light meter which is especially designed for measuring artificial lighting. And here's a few tips. When taking light readings, remember to pick a time of day when it is sunny.

Also, adjust the curtains to their usual daytime position. Drawn curtains, no matter if they are sheer or opaque, can greatly alter the light level so that you won't get a true reading.

Here are some tips from the United States Department of Agriculture, too. For example, when fluorescent tubes become noticeably dim, change them immediately. In standard lamps (400–450 MA) that are operated fifteen hours a day between one and two years, such replacement will be necessary.

Also, some lamps can become dimmer in less time while others may last longer. Keep extra lamps on hand for replacement. Remember that a fixture for two lamps will not operate with just one lamp. Stagger lamp replacement over a period of several weeks to avoid abrupt changes in light level.

Understand, too, that for the first four or five days, new lamps can be up to one-fifth brighter than they will be later on. When applying artificial lights to indoor plants, a general rule is to provide fifteen to twenty watts of light to every square foot of growing space.

Keep in mind that the age of a plant plays a great role in determining how much light intensity it should receive. Seedlings, then, always are in more need of light than mature plants.

# PESTS AND OTHER PLANT AILMENTS

Sometimes insects can cause problems. When this happens, it is best to keep the stricken plant away from the healthy ones. Unless the plant is so far gone with pest festation, there are many products available on the market today that you can easily use to save its life.

Insecticides, for example, are chemical materials used to destroy insects. These come in liquid form and have to be diluted with water. Granules are also made to be mixed with water, and when applied to the ailing plant, its effects are released over a certain period of time whenever you water.

Miticides such as malathion and kelthane are chemicals which are made specifically to destroy mites or spiders. They are mildly to moderately toxic as are any of the insecticides.

For best results, *with any of these products,* follow the manufacturer's instructions to the letter—and with the utmost of care!

A word of caution is necessary at this point. When treating an ailing plant, do it outside the house, especially away from anything edible. Place the treated plant where a child cannot reach it until its harmful effects wear off. An inquisitive toddler would think nothing of taking a bite out of an attractive bit of foliage. Suppose it had been treated?

Pesticides are materials used to eradicate a pest, disease, or any fungus-related problem. They come as wettable powders, liquids, and granules, all of which have to be mixed with water.

Organic pesticides are made without the above-mentioned man-made chemicals. These work by naturally occurring events, by micro-organisms breaking down to present the available matter to the stricken plant. Rotenone, for example, is a product which is derived from plants.

Fungicides are made specifically for fungus-related problems. They, however, are used as a preventative measure and are made to be mixed with water.

What happens here is that little particles float upon the surface of the water. When applied to an ailing plant, a white or gray powdery residue is left. This is the "medicine" that helps make the plant well again. Its effects last from one week to ten days after which the entire procedure should be repeated several times to make sure the health of the plant has been permanently restored.

So far, all the products we have discussed have been applied to plants in such a way that they work to destroy insects from the outside. However, if you leave a plant standing outside, either in the garden or on the porch or patio, rain may easily wash away any previous applications.

Systemics are materials that can enter plants through their roots and foliage and are translocated throughout their inner system. These products come as wettable powders and can also be sprayed on. Excess care must be used when applying systemics because of the high toxic content. Furthermore, if the product is overused it can burn the plant.

The contents of sprays have already been diluted. A

word of caution about using aerosols, though. When applying it to a plant, be sure to hold the can's nozzle no closer than eighteen inches away. If you hold it any closer, the plant's tissues can be burned by the propellant.

You cannot be too careful when it comes to using any of these products. If you feel uncertain as to which of them should be used because you're unsure as to what is wrong with the plant, check with either your local florist, nursery, or County Agricultural Extension Service. Every state has one. Guesswork can only be hazardous to your plant's health.

Pertaining to insects, certain pests are sometimes the cause of particular problems. Mealy bugs, for example, are flat moving insects. They can injure leaves and stems by leaving white cottony masses behind. To get rid of them, wash the plant with a soft toothbrush and warm soapy water. You may also use an insecticide, pyrethrum, or malathion.

Still another thing you can do to get rid of mealy bugs is to dab at them with cotton swabs that have been dipped in rubbing alcohol. Repeat this procedure for the next two or three weeks to make sure that the offspring have all been destroyed. Otherwise, you will wind up with the same problem you had before, maybe worse.

Besides mealy bugs, there are also pests called fungus gnats. They are tiny black insects which fly up when disturbed. First they feed upon dead material in the soil. They they attack the plant's roots. To help solve this problem, water with a solution containing pyrethrum or malathion.

Leaf miners can also be injurious to plants. These

are tiny larvae which burrow in leaves. They cause irregular yellow, cream, or brown-colored channels across foliage. To destroy these pests, use an insecticide spray. Springtails are other types of harmful insects. They are almost transparent jumping bugs that get into the surface of the soil. In addition, they feed on the plant's lower leaves and stems. To destroy them, spray with pyrethrum or malathion. You can also get rid of them by watering with a mild vinegar solution, one to two teaspoons of vinegar to a pint of water.

In speaking about harmful insects, we cannot exclude the mention of thrips. These feed at night and hide by day. They leave thin, papery scars on foliage. To destroy them, spray the plant with a house plant insecticide.

Whiteflies—tiny, white, moth-like insects can also cause trouble. They, like fungus gnats, fly up when they are disturbed. Larvae suck out plant juices and the plant is, understandably, left in a weakened condition. To destroy them, wash the entire plant with warm soapy water. This action will remove wingless larvae. To control the adults, spray with an insecticide.

Aphids are green, red, or black insects which suck the juices from plants. They leave a sticky residue on leaves and stems. In the end, the plant's entire growth is stunted. To destroy aphids, wash the plant with warm water or use rotenone. You may also use an insecticide spray.

Other harmful insects are green or brown scales. They can cluster underneath leaves and on stems. Leaves become mottled from the harmful effects of these pests. To destroy them, carefully scrub the plant's foliage, going over the infected parts with a soft toothbrush and warm soapy water. You may also use an insecticide. Still another method you can prevail upon, is to wipe scales away with cotton swabs that have been dipped in rubbing alcohol. Try a small section of the plant first to see how well it does.

Included among harmful insects are spider mites. They are tiny green, red, or yellowish spiders. They spin fine webs underneath leaves and cause white or yellow spots. Leaves become mottled and dusty-looking. This will make them curl. To destroy these spiders, wash the plant with a soapy warm water solution. Repeat this procedure several times. You may also use an insecticide or miticide. However, in using a spray, after one week has gone by, spray twice more to make certain that these pests have been completely eliminated.

Fungus-related problems usually occur when a plant is exposed to a too-humid atmosphere. These problems can also happen when dead leaves are not removed.

Stem and root rot exhibit blackened stems from the soil up. The plant's roots literally become blackened and begin to decay. At first, the plant will weaken. Eventually, it will die. Should you catch this problem at the onset, dust the healthy parts of the plant such as stems and leaves. Make sure you destroy all infected areas. Use a fungicide and follow the manufacturer's directions.

Another condition referred to as gray mold is justly-named for it attacks the plant with a gray-brown mold. The plant's tissues decay. To save the plant, first destroy all infected parts. Make sure you remove all dead tissue. Then, try to improve air circulation so the plant can breathe easier and heal more quickly. Also use a fungicide.

Sometimes a plant can develop brown leaf spots, which do become quite large. Later, they form moist rot causing first the leaves, and finally, the entire plant to collapse. This condition might not be so easy to cure. Remove all infected areas and improve air circulation. Transfer the plant to a less humid place. If none of these things work, unfortunately, the plant has to be thrown away.

Another fungus-related problem can be found in the form of a powdery mildew. This is a white powder that coats foliage and stems. Eventually, wilting occurs. Transfer the plant to a less humid atmosphere and improve air circulation. Then use a fungicide according to the manufacturer's directions.

You'll notice that I use the words "follow the manufacturer's instructions" very freely, whether it is related to pest/fungus-control problems or fertilizing. Believe me, these words are extremely important and cannot be used often enough.

People, by their very nature, think that if using a little of a particular product brings about satisfactory results, then using twice the amount, if not more, than is specified, will bring quicker results. This is not so. The overuse of any product can only bring about a harmful condition to an otherwise healthy plant. These products are made to promote, not hinder, the healthful status of a plant.

If a plant is too-far-gone, it is understandable that it

must die. However, a plant that requires a simple "shot in the arm" should have no trouble whatsoever in recovering from its mild attack. If, in fact, a plant that has been touched by affliction dies when by all rights it should have recovered, it could have been due to the fault of the product itself, or it could have been misused.

To play it safe, both for you and your plant, *follow the manufacturer's instructions!*

## HOME REMEDIES

In addition to the usual bath of soap and warm water, Eileen Greason, Park Caretaker at the Essex County Park Commission's Center for Environmental Studies in Roseland, New Jersey, recommends placing an ailing plant inside a plastic bag with a no-pest strip. Keep the plant thusly for a period of four days to one week and you will get rid of aphids and whiteflies.

Miss Greason is involved with a home-made remedy that is still in the experimental stage at the Center. Perhaps you might like to try it, too.

Grind up six red hot peppers and a couple of garlic cloves with one cup of water. If you have a blender you can throw all the ingredients into it. Then, strain the solution. It is now ready to be used to spray onto a sick plant. This remedy is designed to get rid of aphids and whiteflies.

# PART 2: FRUITS

# YOUR FIRST PROJECT: THE DATE

Let's start off with the date and grow our own date palm tree. The date palm is considered to be one of the oldest, if not the oldest, cultivated tree known to history. It is even said that it was created from the earth left over from the creation of Adam. Directions for growing this tree have been discovered recorded on sun-baked bricks going back more than five thousand years ago in Mesopotamia.

Interestingly, the date palm, does, in fact, resemble the human for it is either male or female. When grown in orchards in order to bear fruit, pollen from the male must be inserted into the female at just the right time. And once the limb of the tree is severed—that's it. Nothing can be done. A new limb will not grow back to take its place.

During the intense heat of a summer day, the tree's life processes slow down considerably, only to perk up again in the cooler and more comfortable atmosphere of the evening.

The date palm grows in the hot climates of China, Spain, Italy, France, and the southwestern part of the United States. In Algeria, these trees are grown in an oasis where they are planted in deep pits that have been dug into the soil.

The California Date Administrative Committee in Indio, California, advocates the date as a nutritional food as well as a natural sweet. An average date has about twenty-one calories, considerably less than most other snacks—especially candy. It also serves as a good energy booster.

Dates grow in clusters. A single cluster can yield as many as two hundred dates and weigh up to twenty-five pounds. In its natural state, the fruit is more of a golden color, but we are more used to seeing it as dark-brown after it has been processed.

The date is a fleshy and sweet fruit, oblong in shape, with a tough pit inside. However, before you can plant it, make sure to use the unprocessed kind, which can be bought in either a health food store or in the special health food section of your grocery.

Then, after you have eaten the dates, carefully wash the pits under warm running water. Place in containers that have been lined with wet cheesecloth. Be careful not to let the pits get moldy. Wash them again and change the cheesecloth.

If you wish, you can also put the pits into vermiculite that has been covered with plastic wrap. This plastic covering will help keep the pits moist, acting on the same principle as a terrarium. Or, you can plant the pits directly into a mixture containing one part sand or vermiculite, one part soil, and one part humus. Any of these methods will bring satisfactory results. You have but to choose your preference.

Date pits are a little difficult to grow. In that case, to insure a certain amount of survival, plant at least twenty pits. Germination will occur in approximately two months time. A white sprout resembling a toothpick will first appear but eventually this widens out and turns green.

As they grow, pull out any weaker shoots and transplant into separate containers. However, when transplanting, remember that the date has a very deep root system. Make sure that you select a large enough pot to accommodate it.

Thereafter, periodically loosen up the soil by gently digging around the top layer with a fork or spoon. Be careful not to probe too deeply, otherwise you'll injure the plant's delicate roots and they'll die.

Allow the soil to dry out completely between each watering. From then on, when you do water, use just enough to moisten. Never drench it.

Fertilize regularly with one of the commercial plant foods and every so often, add a layer of crushed leaves from your backyard to the soil. This acts as compost, a good additional source of nourishment.

The date palm shuns cold drafts, so taking this into consideration, provide it with the necessary protection it needs. Place in a sunny spot in your home, a south window, preferably.

In the years to come, take pleasure in watching its development. See what you have started from scratch?

# CHERRIES

The cherry, as you know, is a small round fruit that grows on trees. Although many cherries are red in color, the Bing cherry, which is very sweet, is almost black. There are other varieties, too, and they are flesh-colored.

Cherry trees are beautiful in that when in bloom, gorgeous clusters of small white and pink blossoms occur. They grow in the Temperate Zone in such places as Michigan, California, New York, Oregon, Washington, Wisconsin, Pennsylvania, Utah, Idaho, and Ohio.

Sweet cherries are delicious to eat without any preparation, but sour cherries are just that—sour. They can, however, be baked into tempting tarts or pies with the addition of sugar.

Sweet cherry trees are tall and somewhat stout, possessing thick trunks. Their fruit can be black, yellow, or red in color. When fully ripe, they have a deliciously sweet taste. The cold winter weather as well as the hot summer weather can prove harmful to these trees. Like some people, they find it difficult to adjust to extreme weather. Therefore, they are raised in New York State along the eastern shore of Lake Ontario. There, they grow in deep, well-drained soil.

What is interesting about the sweet cherry tree is that it is self-sterile. This means that the pollen from an individual tree cannot pollinate its own flowers. That is why bees are usually kept nearby in the orchard—to help with the pollination.

Sour cherry trees are a little different. For one thing,

they are smaller than the sweet. Secondly, they can survive in either cold or warm climates. They are grown in such places as New York State, California, and Colorado. There, they grow in either light or heavy, well-drained soil. Furthermore, sour cherry trees are self-pollinating since the pollen from one tree can pollinate its own flowers. Interestingly, a single tree can give as much as forty quarts of fruit, which by the way, is a bright red color.

Besides the fact that either sweet or sour cherries can be whipped up into scrumptious desserts, did you ever try eating roast duck with cherry sauce? And did you know that the wild black cherry is the source of cherry brandy and cordials? Is all this talk making you hungry?

Time out to go get some cherries, only this time, hang on to those hard pits. We're going to grow them.

After you have eaten the fruit, rinse the pits, scrubbing off any excess meat. You don't want rotting. Use a toothbrush if necessary. Then place the pits in a plastic bag with a moistened paper towel. Tie the bag closed.

Refrigerate between two-and-a-half to three months. What we're attempting to do here is duplicate the cooler climate from which it comes. At the end of the allotted time, some of the pits may already have cracked open. In case they haven't, crack them open yourself.

Next, choose a container that has adequate drainage and fill it with a regular potting soil mixture. In order to insure a certain amount of survival, plant at least ten cherry pits. Set them an inch deep into the mixture and water lightly.

As the sprouts grow, thin out the weaker ones and

transplant the more sturdy ones into individual pots. In about six or seven months, the seedlings will be approximately twelve inches high.

Keep the soil constantly moist but never let it get too soggy. Overwatering can rot the roots of the plant.

Feed with a commercial fertilizer, making sure to follow the manufacturer's instructions.

Keep in a sunny area of the house. If you wish, permanently transplant out-of-doors during the summer months. The tree *may* produce blossoms and fruit, but it will not necessarily bear the same fruit as its parent variety.

Should aphids occur, wash the plant with warm soapy water. Repeat the procedure to make sure you get rid of all the insects.

# THE MANGO

The mango is an unusual tropical fruit that inhabits the warmer regions of the world. It used to grow wild throughout southeastern Asia as long as four thousand years ago. It wasn't until the 1700s that it was brought over and introduced to the American colonies.

Much has happened since then, for today, Florida alone has cultivated at least fifty different varieties and has contributed greatly in making the mango a more commercial commodity that everyone can enjoy.

The pulp, the edible part of the fruit, is a blazing yellow-orange color. It is indescribably delicious, very soft, and extremely juicy. Inside the meat is a large, hairy pit shaped like a kidney or lima bean. Save this, because with a little know-how, you can plant it and turn it into green foliage.

However, before we begin, a word of caution is necessary here. Believe it or not, the mango is a relative of the poison ivy family. If you are a person who is allergy prone, wear protective gloves to guard against possible skin irritation.

When you are ready to start, scrape away any adhering pulp from the pit. Scrub it throughly with an old toothbrush under warm water. If any meat remains, it will begin to decay and cause the pit to rot.

After the cleansing procedure has been carried out, soak the pit in water for a period of five days. Make certain that you change the water daily.

It is now planting time. With an all-purpose potting soil, place the pit on end, its "eye" facing upward.

Although you can place it with the "eye" down, it is not best. By having it pointing up, the sprout will have a much shorter way to go. In having it face the opposite direction, the sprout will have to take a longer journey. It will grow in the shape of a "U" and will have to go through the bother of first twisting around so that it could poke its way out of the soil. And whatever you do, remember not to lay the pit flat or it will rot.

Cover with a thin layer of soil. If you smoke, by all means, add cigarette ashes to the mixture. The ashes provide an extra source of potassium. (Check chapter four on nutrition)

Then give the soil an initial drenching. As the surface begins to dry, adopt a regular watering routine. Always use warm water and allow the soil to dry out between each watering. Never permit it to become soggy or muddy or the pit can decay.

Once you have planted the pit, don't become alarmed if you don't see immediate results. Patience, which was previously discussed, is required because germination varies from just a few weeks to about four months. At first there will be a pale bare sprout, but this progresses rapidly at the rate of half an inch per day.

When the sprout reaches a height of four inches, shiny, crimson-colored leaves will appear. Expect them to be delicate and droopy at this point.

When the leaves are three inches long, they will turn dark green. Drooping will cease. It is time to cut back those weaker shoots.

This plant, by nature, grows in spurts. Its dormancy

period lasts from four to six weeks. By the end of two years, however, the leaves are going to be a good eight inches long.

To maintain the health of this plant, keep it away from drafty windows, air vents, opening doors, and radiators. Feed with any of the fertilizers, following the manufacturer's instructions, and use only half the recommended dosage.

# THE PEACH

The peach is a truly delicious fruit that people can eat fresh during the summer. However, it can also be enjoyed canned or frozen throughout the winter.

The fruit is round and has a thin, slightly fuzzy skin. Inside its juicy meat is a hard pit. For this reason, the peach is referred to as a stone fruit.

Belief has it that peaches were grown in China more than four thousand years ago. As early as the 1600s, colonists who settled in Virginia grew peach trees. Today, however, peaches are grown in orchards in the United States more than in any other country.

Usually, peach trees grow about twenty-five feet high but growers have to keep them shorter so that they can pick the fruit more easily.

A peach tree has long, slender leaves and blossoms in the spring with beautiful pink flowers. After three years, it will produce fruit.

Fruit growers produce new trees by budding. Buds are taken from a particular tree and set into the lower trunks of seedlings. The tops of the seedlings are cut off after buds have grown onto these trunks and sprouted.

In the south, this procedure is carried out in warm weather so that the trees can be transplanted to orchards in the fall. In the north, the tree is not transplanted until it is two years old.

Peach trees are popularly grown in home gardens. You can plant one too.

After you have eaten the fruit, rinse the hard stone pit thoroughly under warm running water. If any of the juice of the peach remains on the pit, it can ferment, causing the pit to lose its ability to germinate, even if the pit is exposed to this fermenting for as little as twenty-four hours. The pit just won't germinate when planted.

After you have carried out the cleansing procedure, soak the pit for one week. Or, pits, if you intend to plant more than one. Then wrap peach rind around the pits and place two in a gallon milk container that has been filled with one cup of sand, two cups of peat moss, and enough soil, about eight or nine cups, to fill the rest of the carton.

A word of caution: do not pack the soil too tightly. Allow breathing and growing room.

Punch holes in the bottom of the carton to allow for drainage. Then place it outside and set it into the ground as far as it will go. Put stones underneath the container to prevent it from becoming flush against the ground to allow for proper drainage.

Cover the top with leaves and twigs for warmth and moisture over the cold winter months. If possible, use oak leaves, as they supply a sufficient amount of acid to the soil.

In the event that you are using more than one carton with which to plant a large number of pits, space them two to three inches apart. Camphor placed strategically around the area will help keep insects away.

Germination takes about six to seven months, so be patient. Later, when branches become numerous, prune the newer ones to let air and light penetrate and deter branches from blocking each other's growth. Paint balm over the cuts.

The tree, if it is going to bear fruit at all, will do so in two to three years.

You may also plant the pit indoors. To do so, wash the juice off with warm running water. Then soak it at room temperature for three days, changing the water daily, rinsing the pit thoroughly each time. Nick the hard outer shell with a file to speed up germination.

To plant, select a four-inch pot with adequate drainage. Fill with an all-purpose potting mixture and set the pit about an inch and a half deep.

Germination cannot be hurried and will take many months. Keep soil evenly moist at all times and keep pot in a sunny location. When you get an actively growing plant, feed with any of the plant foods, following the manufacturer's directions.

At the beginning of the peach season, you may come across many split pits. The seed inside the hard covering will be exposed. Planting the seed thusly is a hit or miss affair, because there's a chance it could be sterile. Unfortunately, there is no sure way in which to tell whether or not the seed is viable.

Many of these split pits don't germinate for various reasons, one in particular, because the fruit could be old. If germination doesn't occur inside of two months, start the project over again. You might have better luck next time. Otherwise, stay with the hard stone pit and simply wait out its long germinating period.

# THE PLUM

The plum is what is known as a stone fruit, in that inside its flesh is a hard, stone-like pit. It grows in temperate regions and comes in all different shapes and sizes—colors, too, for the thin skin can be green, purple, red, yellow, even blue.

Plums grow on small trees. When they bloom, greenish-white flowers appear. It is unusual because these flowers blossom before the leaves do.

Plums first made their debut in Europe over two thousand years ago around the Caucasus Mountains and the Caspian Sea. They were first introduced to America in the early 1600s. However, the fruit didn't really gain in popularity here until the 1700s, when they began to be planted in quantity.

Another interesting fact to point out is that as early as the 1500s, it was discovered, in Hungary, how to dry plums and make them into prunes. Today, it is a very important product which can commonly be found in any neighborhood supermarket. Prunes, by the way, are made by breaking the skin of the plums. They are then placed in the sun to dry.

There's no denying that plums taste delicious. They are very high in nutritional value in comparison to some other fruit. Most of the time, plums are eaten fresh. However, they also make good eating in the form of jams, jellies, and preserves.

The next time you eat a plum, save the pit. Wash it thoroughly under warm running water. Use an old toothbrush to scrub away any adhering flesh. If any of the meat is allowed to remain, it could rot and cause the entire pit to decay.

After you have cleaned the pit, place it, or as many as you wish to use, in a plastic bag along with moistened paper toweling. Tie the bag securely and refrigerate for ninety days. Remember, the plum grows in a cool climate, and we want to simulate the environment in which it is used to living.

At the end of ninety days, remove the pit from the refrigerator and the plastic bag. By that time, some of the pits may have opened up by themselves. Those that have not should be opened with a nutcracker or a file. Be careful not to harm the inner seed of the hard pit.

Place in a regular potting mixture about an inch deep. Use a four-inch pot as a starter. Germination will occur within a month.

Keep the soil constantly moist, never dry or soggy. Place in a sunny spot in your home.

You may, if you wish, transplant in the garden during the summer. It is doubtful you'll get fruit. However, there's the *possibility* that the plant will produce blossoms and fruit in the third year.

Feed with fish emulsion following the manufacturer's directions.

# THE PERSIMMON

The persimmon is an unusual fruit that is oriental by heritage. However, for commercial purposes, the fruit is grown here in the United States in southern California.

Persimmons grow on trees. There are male trees and female trees, so it is impossible to pollinate the flowers yourself to get fruit.

And speaking of the fruit, when you buy it in the supermarket, usually in the fall, you will find that the shape and size of it is similar to that of the tomato. The skin is smooth to the touch.

When the persimmon is ripe, it has a yellowish color, but if it isn't, the color is somewhat green. Although you can eat the fruit raw, be careful about biting into an unripe one. You won't like it. Your mouth will pucker with a very strange sensation. You can prevent the fruit from yielding such unpleasantness by placing it into warm water for a long spell or by putting it in the freezer. When eating a ripened persimmon, notice how the high sugar content enhances the flavor of the fruit.

Next time you eat a persimmon, hang on to those seeds. Rinse them in a closely-meshed strainer under warm running water. Dry by rolling them gently between paper toweling.

After that, place the seeds into a plastic bag along with some sphagnum moss. Refrigerate this way for three months, making sure the bag is tied securely.

At the end of that time, using five or six seeds to

insure some survival, plant them an inch deep in a regular potting soil mixture. Check the container for adequate drainage. Germination will occur from two to ten weeks.

When the first true leaves appear, they will have a shine to them. These leaves will change in appearance as soon as the first truly mature leaves bloom.

In approximately six months, the plant will be between two and four inches high. Time to pinch back the plant. When it is about one year old, it will have reached a height of six to eight inches tall. A slow, but steady grower.

The persimmon plant requires good sun, preferably a southern exposure.

Water well when you water, but water again only when the top layer of soil begins to dry out. Keep it constantly moist, never too dry, never soggy.

Feed with a water soluble fertilizer according to the manufacturer's directions.

# THE GUAVA

Yes, you're reading the title correctly. This chapter is, indeed, on the guava. Perhaps you'd like to know a few things about this tropical fruit.

The guava is a fruit that flourishes in the warm climates of California, Florida, and Brazil. There, it grows on small trees. When they bloom, pretty little white flowers appear, much like the way cherry trees do.

Guavas are not particularly large, only about the size of an egg. Some are shaped like a pear while others are more rounded. The fruit has a grainy texture somewhat reminiscent of the pear's. If you've never eaten one before, this comparison gives you a pretty good description.

One thing about guavas, though. They have an unusual smell. Kind of skunky, or musky. They taste the same way, too. This is a fruit that you might have to develop a taste for, the same way you would for olives.

The fruit has an attractive red color to it, although there are guavas that are also yellow.

Guavas can be used in a number of ways. Perhaps you already know about guava jelly. However, you can also stew the fruit on top of the stove the same way you would an apple or prunes. In addition, you can eat it as a dessert or sliced fresh and served with cream.

Now that we've learned something about the guava, it is time to plant the pit, but first you must rinse it thoroughly under warm running water.

It is up to you, but you can let it soak for a few days

at room temperature, changing the water daily, or you may plant it immediately. Either way, you will get it growing.

Select a container with adequate drainage and fill it with an all-purpose potting mixture. Place the seed, then cover with a thin layer of the soil, about a quarter of an inch or so.

Germination will occur between three to six weeks. As growth progresses, suckers will grow from the bottom part of the plant. Because they only serve to weaken, take them off.

This is a plant that loves warmth, so keep it in a sunny location in your house. A southern exposure is best.

In the summer, don't let the direct rays of the sun hit the plant. Protect it with a drawn sheer curtain.

The guava's natural growing process is straight up. Because bushing it out is not necessary here, you don't have to bother with pruning.

You probably won't get fruit but you'll wind up with a lovely foliage plant. Just water well when you water, keeping the soil evenly moist. When you notice the top layer of soil beginning to dry, water.

Feed with any house plant food using the dosage that the manufacturer recommends, following exact instructions.

# THE PAPAYA

Now that we are making such good progress, let's continue with the papaya.

The papaya is an exotic fruit that grows in tropical countries. It grows on a small palm-like plant and is roughly round in shape. Yellow-orange in color, the papaya has a sweet, slightly musky flavor.

In its native habitat, the papaya, when it is ripe, can be eaten straight off the tree. However, the fruit can also be picked when it is only half-ripe so that it can be cooked with sugar to make preserves.

But the papaya is much more than just a delicious fruit. It is also the source of a drug called papain. Papain is something which is very similar to pepsin, a substance which aids in the digestion of food. In addition, papain is used to soften tough cuts of meat before they are cooked. This can be valuable when cutting down on food expenses, for it enables the housewife to save by allowing her to purchase less expensive cuts of meat which she can tenderize with the papain.

Recently, papaya has taken another big climb in popularity. In fact, the next time you go to the supermarket, take notice of the bottles of papaya juice sitting on top of the shelves. Not only that, the next time you go shopping in one of the malls, stop in at one of the health food stores and treat yourself to a glass of ice-cold papaya juice. It is extremely refreshing and low in calories. The price is right, too! Speaking from experience, papaya juice is a real "pick-me-up" when you are at your lowest ebb.

With the papaya, you will find, that when you cut the fruit open, the broader end has a hole in it—like a squash—and this hole is loaded with hundreds of small black seeds. Don't throw them away because when you plant them, you will eventually wind up with beautiful green foliage. In the years to come, it will grow into a handsome tree, just the right height to be able to display it in your living room as part of the decor.

Just follow these simple instructions and you're on your way. Remove the seeds from the fruit. Place them in a strainer. Then, with your hand, rub the seeds against the wire mesh while running them under warm running water to remove the aril. Aril is a slippery coating which acts as a protective covering for the seed out in the wild. It turns hard to protect the seed through dry conditions until the time is right for germination. When the time is right, it moistens, turning into the slippery coating you must now wash off. With the cleansing procedure carried out and the aril removed, permit the seeds to dry out for one day.

As a rule, you do not require a large container for a tiny plant, but in the case of the papaya, it is necessary. It is not so much that the papaya loves space, but that it does not take too kindly to being transplanted. Therefore, select a pot that has sufficient drainage, clay preferably, because of its porosity, and large enough, because it will be the plant's permanent home.

Fill with an all-purpose potting mixture. Then, using the tip of a pencil, poke quarter-inch holes and place your seeds. To insure a certain amount of survival, start at least twelve. Germination takes place anywhere from one to six weeks. As you can see, a little patience is needed.

When sprouts are two inches high, pinch back the weaker ones. Continue pinching back until you are left with one truly healthy plant.

Until the plant is at least three inches tall, do not give it more than one hour of direct sunlight each day because the leaves can burn.

Mist daily, but when you do, mist either early in the morning or late in the day. For added humidity, keep the papaya plant in the bathroom or laundry room. Whenever you bathe, the steamy atmosphere will create an ideal environment for it in which to live.

Feed with one of the commercial plant foods and follow the formulator's directions.

Here's an interesting note: Did you know that the papaya plant is very susceptible to air pollution, especially to ethylene which is contained in auto exhausts?

Gas mask, anyone?

# THE APPLE

Way back in history, the people of ancient Rome took great pride in the growing of apple trees. Word has it that when they conquered England, they introduced the fruit there. From then on, other European countries began planting apple trees, too.

It wasn't until the early 1600s that apples were introduced to America. History's grapevine has it that John Endicott, the governor of the Massachusetts Bay Colony, was the one to have brought the first trees to America. Different varieties then began to spread over the land.

When the popularity of apples began to take on dimension, Indians removed the seeds from the fruit and planted them in the wilderness and in their villages.

A man by the name of John Chapman used to carry apple seeds with him wherever he went. He continued doing this until one day even the most sparsely populated areas of America became dotted with apple trees. Because he did this, John Chapman earned the nickname, "Johnny Appleseed."

Apples have led a romantic life. They are mentioned in legends and poems. And although the name of the fruit that Adam and Eve were supposed to have eaten in the Garden of Eden was not actually mentioned, the fruit is said by all to have been the apple.

In a legend pertaining to the Greeks, a golden apple was the object that was the cause of a terrible quarrel among the gods, leading to the destruction of Troy.

And what about when William Tell was supposed to

have taken a bow and arrow so he could shoot the apple off his son's head?

Then there's the expression, "as American as apple pie."

Today, the United States leads the way as an apple-producing country. The fruit is grown in cool regions and are usually raised in orchards.

There are, of course, many, many varieties, all delicious to eat. However, not only are apples scrumptious, they are nutritious and aid in digestion.

The next time you bite into an apple, don't swallow those seeds. Save them and plant them. They are easy to germinate, a good project for those who like something easy to try.

Remove the seeds from the fruit and rinse them in a strainer under warm running water. Then soak them in water overnight at room temperature.

The next day, drain and place the moistened seeds into a sealed plastic bag. Chill in the refrigerator for forty-five days. Remember, apples come from cool regions and this procedure is to duplicate their home environment.

At the end of the forty-five days, remove the seeds from the bag and press them slightly into a moist potting soil mixture so that the seeds are just below the soil's surface. Place a glass or a piece of plastic over the container until the seeds germinate. Germination will occur between thirty to sixty days.

When the seedlings are a few inches tall, transfer into individual pots. Maintain the soil at a moist level and feed with fish emulsion, following the manufacturer's directions.

Keep in a sunny part of the house but avoid direct sunlight. After two years, you may, if you wish, transplant outdoors in a sunny location.

"Apple varieties," explains Fred P. Corey, Director of the International Apple Institute in Washington, D.C., "do not propogate true to parentage from seed.

"If the seedlings are grown to fruiting age, the fruit will not be of any particular predictable size, shape, or color. They may or may not resemble the parent variety."

In continuing, Mr. Corey states: "After two or three years from seed, if a particular variety is desired, a live bud of that variety may be grafted or budded onto the stem or trunk of the small seedling.

"When the bud 'takes' and starts to grow, after one growing season, cut off the original seedling tree just above the variety bud. The budded growth will then become the new apple tree."

# THE KIWI

Yes, I know, the kiwi is a bird, but not in this case. We are, of course, referring to an edible object, for the kiwi is a very unusual fruit. It is raised commercially in New Zealand and California. Interestingly, the kiwi grows much in the same way that grapes grow, on a vine. And like grapes, kiwis can be trellised. They can also be grown on an arbor.

Alas, because there is a female kiwi plant and a male kiwi plant, there will be no fruit. Besides, when we buy the fruit, there is no way to know which one is the boy and which one is the girl.

However, even if we can't mate a couple of kiwis to bear fruit, it is still enjoyable to eat. It is a little difficult to describe the flavor of a kiwi but when chewing it, you will notice that it has the same grainy texture common to strawberries.

The next time you go to your supermarket, search out the kiwi. You can't miss it. It's egg-shaped and is chartreuse in color. The skin is very thin. Hairy, too, and somewhat on the rough side. Altogether, it makes a pretty unusual appearance.

When I ate it, I cut off the top of the fruit and scooped out the pulp with a spoon. It was a beautiful pale green color. The next time *you* cut open a kiwi, save those tiny seeds. We're going to plant them. Here's how.

Rinse the seeds carefully in a closely-meshed strainer under warm running water. Then let them dry out overnight.

Next morning, place the seeds in a plastic bag along with some dampened sphagnum moss. Fasten the bag securely with a tie and store in the refrigerator for forty days.

If you wish, however, after the seeds have dried, place them on top of soil that has been layered with dampened milled sphagnum moss. Over the seeds, place still another layer of the moistened sphagnum. The reason behind this is to try and avoid damping off. This term refers to a fungi that lives at soil level, and there, attacks germinating seedlings. Although seedlings are much more resistant to damping off when they reach a certain age, the procedure just mentioned should be used as a preventative or precautionary measure.

In any event, whichever method you choose to start your plants growing, transplant the sprouts to larger and individual containers when they are three to four inches high.

Adopt a regular watering routine, keeping the soil evenly moist. Train vines to grow up a trellis.

This plant is comfortable with a southern exposure but guard against a too direct sun. You don't want any leaves to burn.

When the plant is actively growing, feed with any of the plant foods out on the market and carefully follow the manufacturer's instructions. However, start out using a quarter of the recommended strength, building slowly to half, then full.

# GRAPES

Grapes are one of history's oldest cultivated plants. As a matter of fact, you will find the mention of grapes in the Bible, in myths, and in fairy tales.

Remember the story about the fox and the crow? The cunning fox tried everything in the book to try to get the bird, who was perched high out of reach on the branch of a tree, to relinquish the delicious-looking grape from its beak.

In the end, the fox, after failing every tactic he employed, decided to give it one more good old college try. He flattered the crow so much, that the bird became overwhelmed. It tried to thank the fox and in doing so, opened its beak. Naturally, the grape fell—right into the waiting open mouth of the sly animal.

Who can blame the fox for desiring the grape so badly, because the fruit is juicy and delicious. It is grown in temperate regions such as California, New York, Washington, and Michigan. Grapes are used to make wine, juice, and are dried into the raisins you see in your cereal.

There are thousands of varieties of grapes. Before they became popular here in America, they grew wild in the southern part of Europe, North Africa, and in the southeastern part of Asia.

When they were finally introduced here, there were weather problems. Either the winters were much too cold in the north, or else the summers were way too hot for the grapes in the south. Later, it was discovered that California was an ideal place in which to grow them.

Popular are the green seedless grapes that we see in our supermarkets when the season becomes warmer. There are also green seeded grapes, which are somewhat large and firm. In addition to these varieties are the red and purple, which can be enjoyed straight from the fruit bowl.

Grapes grow in an interesting way on woody vines in orchards. The vineyears of certain European countries such as France and Italy are very well-known for raising grapes for champagne.

And now, let's grow some lovely plants from the seeds of grapes. The next time you eat the fruit, save the seeds and rinse them well in a strainer under warm running water. Then let them dry out overnight.

Or, if you prefer, you can also plant them immediately in a container that has been filled with a mixture of one part sand or vermiculite, one part soil, and one part humus. To insure some survival, plant ten seeds to one pot.

After they have been planted, cover them with an extra eighth of an inch of humus. When the sprouts are six inches high, add still another quarter of an inch of humus. Crumble up some leaves from your backyard in there, too.

As growth progresses, thin out the weaker shoots. It is also time to use a trellis to train the vines. Since vining is the plant's natural growing pattern, as previously mentioned, it will die if it is not allowed to grow horizontally.

While they are still very young, do not give the vines more than two hours of sun each day or they will burn.

As growth slows with impending dormancy, cut them back ten or twelve inches. Dormancy is a very peculiar situation with the grape. It could last for as long as five months. The plant might not show signs of life all during this time so don't become alarmed. It didn't die. It's only resting.

It's not temperature that triggers this dormancy period, it's light duration, or the length of the day. When spring returns, bringing with it much longer days, growth will begin again.

When dormancy occurs, water on a less frequent basis. When growth resumes, maintain a regular watering routine as always. Keep the soil barely moist and feed with one of the plant foods at the recommended dosage.

# THE POMEGRANATE

Pomegranates grow wild in hot countries such as western Asia and northwestern India. Although they grow in a bushlike fashion out in the wild, they can, however, be cultivated into small trees for commercial purposes, such as they are here in the southern part of the United States.

The fruit is round and red in color. It has a tough, thick rind that covers a tasty crimson-colored pulp. This pulp is used in the making of refreshing drinks. The Iranians use it to make wine. The rind contains a substance called tannin. It is used in medicine as well as for tanning leather. In addition, we get grenadine syrup from the fruit.

The pomegranate was found, interestingly enough, pictured on the pillars of Solomon's Temple. It also has a fascinating mythological story, too. One day, Proserpina, who was the daughter of Ceres, goddess of agriculture, was out picking flowers, when Pluto broke his way up through the earth in a black chariot and whisked her to his Lower World kingdom. There, he made Proserpina his Queen.

Ceres was terribly worried because she couldn't find her daughter. She let all her duties go and crops all over the world began to die. The only thing that was on her mind was her missing daughter.

Finally, after much searching, she found out where Proserpina was. Ceres sent a message to Pluto to let her daughter go if her daughter had not eaten any food in the underworld.

Pluto was sly for he had given Proserpina a pomegranate to eat. When she was eating it, she accidentally swallowed six seeds from the fruit. From then on, Proserpina was forced to live with Pluto in his kingdom for six months every year. She was, however, allowed to live with her mother for the other six months.

Every time Proserpina had to leave for the underworld kingdom, her mother mourned the entire time she was gone. The crops foundered and died. With her return, Ceres tended to the earth once more. Legend has it that because of this event, we get the change of seasons.

The next time you eat a pomegranate, remember this story and be careful not to swallow any of those seeds. Instead, save them and plant them. Here's how.

When you cut open the pomegranate, you will find many small seeds inside. Remove them from the fruit, rinse in a strainer under warm running water to wash away the slippery coating, then dry for several days.

Next, put the seeds into a closed container that has been lined with moistened cheesecloth. Mold might occur, but it's nothing to be concerned about. You don't have to change the cheesecloth, either.

If you prefer, you may place the seeds in a shallow pan that has been filled with vermiculite and cover with plastic wrap. Keep the seeds warm and moist.

In about six weeks the seeds will crack open. A small tap root will appear. Select a container that has adequate drainage and fill it with one part sand or vermiculite, one part soil, and one part humus.

Using a pencil, poke quarter-inch deep holes. Rinse the seeds and place in the holes, root side down. Water lightly. In two weeks shoots will poke their way through the soil.

This plant does not like too much humidity, nor does it like to be misted. As a matter of fact, it's perfect for those hard-to-grow spots because it likes a hot and dry atmosphere.

Contrary to the usual instructions on plant care, you can even keep this plant on top of a radiator. A word of caution, however, if you do, and that is to water more often. Do not let the roots get so dry as to wither and die.

In a few years, pinkish-red blossoms will appear. If you want the plant to bear fruit, you might have to pollinate it yourself. To do this, simply take a cotton swab or a soft paint brush and dab gently in each flower.

Fertilize regularly with a commercial house plant food and follow the formulator's instructions.

# THE PRICKLY PEAR

Can you imagine growing the seeds from a prickly pear? Well, that's what we're going to do. Just *stick* with me, okay?

There's a cactus that grows in the dry regions of northern Mexico and the southwestern part of the United States. It is referred to as Nopal, or Indian fig. This cactus bears many prickly fruits that are shaped like a pear or a fig.

Prickly pears are raised in Florida, Brazil, South Africa, India, the Canary Islands, and Madagascar.

The prickly pear is noted for its food value and is also used in the dye industry. How unusual it is that the fruit is planted on Mount Vesuvius after a flow of lava has cooled. There, roots grow easily in the cracks of rocks. A great deal has been accomplished here, for in growing the prickly thusly, it has helped make the earth a more suitable ground in which other plants can live.

While the fruit is growing, it develops prickly spines. They are removed by a process called singeing. You might take notice the next time you go to the supermarket, the stubbly part is left over after the spines have been removed.

As a matter of fact, spineless varieties have been developed, but if a really bad drought happens along, the spiny kind is fed to livestock.

The prickly pear is a beautiful red color. The fruit is rather small in size, but is very tasty to eat. It can be cut up with other fruit and served as a compote. Upon slicing it open, you will find many small black seeds.

You know what we're going to do with them, don't you? Of course, grow them!

Here's how.

Remove the seeds from the thick end of the fruit and rinse them thoroughly. Let them dry for two days. Germinate them in the pot you want them to grow in because they do not take to transplanting.

Germinating seedlings are prone to a fungi that attacks at soil level. Therefore, precautionary measures have to be taken.

Spread a layer of a composition containing one part sand or vermiculite, one part soil, and one part humus in a pot. Add a quarter of an inch layer of dampened milled sphagnum moss, the seeds of the fruit, and finally, another quarter of an inch layer of the moistened sphagnum moss.

Water heavily. Then keep the soil constantly moist but never allow it to become soggy or muddy.

Germination will occur within four to six weeks. The first shoot will not look like much—just two thick leaves on a stem. About two weeks later, thin white hairs will develop on the juncture of the leaves, followed by a barrel-shaped cacti joint with white hairy bristles.

Very often, the seed will sprout two shoots. Since the first shoot is the stronger, it will take over in a few months. Therefore, pinch it off now.

This plant requires plenty of sun. In fact, it is a good idea to begin it in warmer weather. Water just enough to keep the soil moist. Let it dry out between each watering. Never let it become muddy or soggy.

Feed with one of the commercial plant foods and follow the manufacturer's directions.

# THE PINEAPPLE

At one time, the pineapple was an epiphytic plant, that is, it had no roots and lived in the crooks of trees. As it evolved through the ages, a drastic change took place. No longer was it an air plant. No longer did it grow in the nooks of trees. It began to grow by means of a root system, which is the way the pineapple grows today.

The Spaniards first introduced the pineapple to South America after a series of explorations. A man named John Evelyn wrote in his diary about having eaten pineapple from Barbados when he dined with Charles II at his home in England. In those early days, pineapples were considered such a delicacy that they were only grown privately in English gardens.

The pineapple is so-named because of its great resemblance to the pine cone. Depending upon where it comes from, it can take on various shapes and sizes. Of course, the most famous pineapple-growing places are Hawaii and Puerto Rico, but pineapples also come from Florida, Jamaica, the Bahamas, and Trinidad.

It is safe to say that pineapples, no matter where you get them from, are exquisitely delicious, for the meat, when allowed to fully ripen, is extremely sweet and juicy. Sometimes you are almost positive that it had been dipped in sugar.

In handling a pineapple, you have to be careful, because the leaves are spiny. You can usually tell if the fruit is ready to eat if you can pull out one of the center leaves easily. Another way to tell is by sniffing. If you detect a strong, sweet aroma, it is time to cut the pineapple open. Also, the outside should take on a brownish or yellowish cast.

The pineapple cannot be grown from seed. It has to be propagated by planting its crown. Next time you eat a pineapple, here's what to do:

Cut the crown, or tuft of leaves, off the fruit, leaving about an inch of the fruit still attached. Let this sit and rest for a day or two so that the wound can scab or heal.

Then bury the fruit portion in a mixture of half soil, a quarter humus, and a quarter coffee grounds. That's right, coffee grounds. They supply an abundance of acidity to the soil.

Once you have perked your coffee, rinse the grounds in a strainer under warm running water. Then bake in the oven at two hundred and fifty degrees for an hour or until the grounds dry out.

After you have planted the crown you may get some new shoots. You might get a ratoon which grows out of the soil and has roots, or you might get an aerial sucker which doesn't have roots.

When small shoots have grown about a dozen healthy leaves, separate them carefully from the parent and start rooting them.

Interestingly, the pineapple plant will bear fruit outdoors after two years, but it will not bear fruit indoors unless you place an apple in with it. As the apple rots, the decaying matter gives off a certain gas that is necessary in order for germination to occur.

Keep your pineapple plant in the warmest place possible because it needs all the sun it can get. A southern exposure is ideal. If temperatures drop below sixty-five degrees, the plant can go dormant, so supply as much direct sunlight as you can.

However, if temperatures rise to over ninety degrees, the plant will have excessive transpiration. Too much oxygen and too much water is an unhealthy condition for the plant.

The pineapple plant can receive nutrition through its leaves. Therefore, fertilize with one of the commercial fertilizers cutting the recommended dose to one-quarter. Use it twice as often as the instructions indicate. You can also spray food directly onto the plant's leaves. Just be aware that it is unsafe to do this with other house plants.

Use food that is sequestered, one that is high in iron content. Do not use one with too much phosphate or sodium compound in it.

Watch for browning leaves, a sign that you're fertilizing too much. To adjust, dilute the plant food and use it less often.

# THE BANANA

In case you are blinking twice, let me assure you that yes, indeed, this chapter is on how to grow a banana plant. We've come this far and anything is possible in this book, as I'm sure you must know by now.

Bananas grow in jungles where the environment is hot and damp. Although they originated in Asia, other tropical countries have been cultivating them, too, Central America ranking highest as the most important of the banana-producing countries.

The plant, itself, is very tall, reaching a height of about twenty-five feet. It grows in a most unusual manner in that long stalks of leaves wrap around each other in such a tight way, that eventually it becomes a long, stiff bundle. The overall appearance is that of a thick tree trunk, but that's all it is—a similarity—for the banana plant is not a tree.

It takes a banana plant approximately fifteen months to reach full maturity. At that time, large clusters of flower buds appear. Inside their petals are small flowers that later turn into tiny green bananas.

As growth continues, more flowers will grow and then more bananas appear, and this pattern keeps repeating itself until many, many more bananas have formed.

There are a great many varieties of bananas. Some are even inedible. We here in the United States are used to seeing the common large, yellow, smooth-skinned kind in the supermarket.

The longer you allow a banana to ripen, the browner

its peel turns and the sweeter the fruit becomes. Most people aren't aware that the peel is extremely protective toward the banana for it is both dirt-proof and germproof, a comforting thought, indeed.

Let me caution you about this particular chapter for it is going to be a little different from the rest. The reason I have chosen it is because it makes a spectacular project, for when was the last time you grew a banana plant in your home?

There are two types of bananas that we eat, seeded and unseeded. If we eat the seedless variety, naturally there are no seeds for us to grow. If we eat the seeded kind, those seeds are sterile. Therefore, they cannot be germinated.

As you can tell this presents a problem. That is why, for this project, we have to cheat a bit. Look for further explanation at the end of this chapter. Meanwhile, we'll take it from here.

To prepare banana seeds for planting, nick or scratch them first. Then let them soak at room temperature overnight.

Next day, place seeds nicked side up in a combination of two-third's humus to one-third soil. Cover with a quarter of an inch of this mixture.

Here is a perfect opportunity to practice patience because germination is extremely erratic. It can take anywhere from one week to four months.

When the plant is actively growing, maintain the soil at a very moist level and, most important, keep it warm. Give it full sun as often as possible. Provide underneath heat by placing the plant on top of an electrical appliance.

Place a thermometer into the soil to keep tabs on the amount of warmth that the plant is receiving. An ideal temperature should read between eighty to eighty-five degrees.

Most likely you won't get bananas but at least you'll end up with attractive foliage.

However, if by some chance seeds do set to produce fruit, the banana plant will send off a gas called ethylene. Ethylene protects the plant while it is living in the wild and while it is fine over there, it could harm your other plants and your goldfish at home. For this reason it would be best to separate the banana plant from all others.

Feed with a water soluble fertilizer every week, using only half the recommended dosage.

Now for the seeds. To obtain them they must be sent for. They are very interesting to look at once they have been received. They are nugget-like and brown with a hard, shell-like covering. Before planting them, nick each with a file.

Banana seeds can be ordered at this address for a small charge. Write to:

George W. Park Seed Co., Inc.
P. O. Box 31
Greenwood, South Carolina 29647

Have fun!

# CITRUS

When talking about citrus, we are referring to such fruits as the orange, the grapefruit, the lemon, the lime, the tangerine, and other citrus varieties.

A point of interest lies in the fact that the Chinese were the first people to cultivate citrus trees as early as 1000 B.C., but of course, as you well know, citrus is now grown in other parts of the world.

Citrus fruits grow on trees and shrubs. Ranking high in its production are Florida and California, for these states can well supply the sun that citrus trees require.

If you've ever received a gift of oranges and grapefruits from Florida, you can't help but notice the superior quality of the fruit. Oranges derived from other sources are more or less puny. You have to squeeze many oranges in order to get a small glass of juice. However, you have only to squeeze a single Florida orange, and you not only get a large glass of juice, but the taste is exquisite.

The next time you squeeze oranges for juice, or the next time you use a lemon or a lime, or the next time you serve your family grapefruit halves, save the seeds. I, myself, have planted a large number of tangerine seeds. It was easy to do. In fact, I started so many, that I kept one plant and gave the rest to the experimental station in Roseland, New Jersey.

A woman I met has a grapefruit tree in her den that she started eighteen years ago. Today, the tree is seven feet tall. She also has a five-foot lemon tree that she started from the seeds of the fruit. None of her trees have fruit, but there was an item in the newspaper about a woman whose lemon tree bore lemons after fifteen years. So you never know!

However, it is time to begin our project. First rinse the seeds from any citrus fruit in a strainer under warm running water. Then let them soak overnight. Then, set the seeds into a composition containing one part sand or vermiculite, one part soil, and one part humus. Cover the seeds with half an inch of this mixture. Then water.

To insure some survival, plant at least two dozen seeds. Germination takes place in about one month. At first small sprouts will appear, then tiny vivid green leaves. Mist them daily. Never let them dry out or they will wilt and die. Remove weak sprouts.

When the shoots are about five inches tall, transplant them into separate containers. Later, as growth progresses, you'll be able to catch the pleasant citrusy fragrance by rubbing the leaves between your fingers.

In repotting a citrus, be careful not to disturb the old soil adhering to the root of the plant. Always fill the new container with a partial amount of the original potting mixture. This helps the plant make a better adjustment to its new environment.

Periodically bathe the plant with warm water or wash the leaves with a moistened cloth. Otherwise, clinging dust can bring about insects. Because you should never use a household insect spray on a citrus plant, keeping its leaves clean is the best preventative measure there is to ward off unwanted pests.

The citrus plant requires a great deal of sun so keep it in a southern exposure.

Fertilize with a water soluble plant food about every four or five weeks following the manufacturer's instructions. When the plant maintains its dark green color, all is well. Should it become somewhat pale, correct the situation with fertilizer. Its richness will return.

Sometimes, when growing citrus in the home, the plant can become scraggly. When this happens, prune the plant heavily, cutting the top back about one-third. Do not worry that you are taking too much off the plant because you aren't. Notice, instead, how much bushier the foliage becomes. After this extensive pruning, however, hold off on fertilizing until fresh growth has appeared.

There's one more thing to point out. The citrus plant will have thorns, so if you have any small inquisitive children about, take care that they don't prick their little fingers on them.

# THE HONEYDEW MELON

You may consider this chapter a little unusual for it deals with growing a plant from, of all things, honeydew seeds. However, the purpose of this book is to introduce you to projects you never thought possible.

The honeydew, with which we are all well acquainted, is a viny fruit that is large and round, possessing a smooth rind. Inside is a delicious, green, sweet, juicy flesh.

In early times, honeydews were first grown in India. Later they were introduced and produced in Asia and Egypt. Also, the melon was a popular favorite among the ancient Romans and Greeks. In America, it has been cultivated since colonial days and was grown commercially for the first time around the 1890s.

According to the Essex County Park Commission's Center for Environmental Studies in Roseland, New Jersey, you can grow a beautiful hanging plant from the seeds of this melon.

However, because this fruit *is* a warm-weather treat, best results can be attained by starting the seeds in late April or mid May, after the last frost days.

Here's how to do it. To begin, select a five-inch container. Fill with a regular potting mix.

Build a mound with the soil and in it, place five honeydew seeds. Set them a quarter to about half an inch deep, then cover with a thin layer of the mixture. Water just enough to dampen.

Germination will take place within two weeks. When sprouts appear, and the plant is actively growing, you can either train them to grow up a trellis—because if you'll remember, by nature, the honeydew grows on vines—or use it as a hanging plant.

As growth continues, the plant will develop attractive, somewhat rounded leaves along with pretty yellow flowers. Since this is a sun-loving plant, place in a south window so that the flowers can bloom to full capacity.

Adopt a regular watering routine and feed with a water soluble fertilizer about every two weeks, following the manufacturer's directions.

You must realize that planting honeydew seeds indoors and confining them to pots will grow a good-looking plant, but you won't get fruit. However, if you want fruit, select a good sunny location in your outdoor garden. Mound some soil and place your seeds.

When growing the seeds out-of-doors, you can expect insects. To get rid of them, use an organic spray such as rotenone.

# THE AVOCADO

Something would be missing if I didn't include our friend the avocado, so here it is.

The avocado is a fruit that grows on trees that are part of the laurel family. Sometimes it is also called the *alligator pear*. Avocados need a warm climate in which to grow and California and Florida lead the way.

The avocado is a large fruit and can weigh up to three pounds. It comes in various shapes, too. Round, ovate, and even bottle-shaped. Color can vary, too, from green to very dark purple.

A tough, leathery skin surrounds an extremely soft, yellow-green pulp. This pulp is the edible portion of the fruit and has a slightly nutty flavor.

Inside the avocado is a large, pear-shaped pit. After you have eaten the fruit, whether it be sliced into a delicious salad, or mashed into an equally delicious Guacomole dip, save this pit for planting.

Use the pit of a good, ripe avocado. The fruit is ripe if, when squeezed, it feels soft.

To begin, scrub the pit with a toothbrush under warm running water. Do not allow any adhering meat to remain because once that starts to rot, the entire pit can decay.

After the pit has been rinsed, let it dry overnight. Next day, insert three or four toothpicks horizontally into the pit, about two-thirds of the way up its sides.

With the toothpicks placed firmly enough to support the pit, suspend it over a jar, its pointed end facing up, one-third submerged in water.

Keep the water fresh. Change it every week, replenishing it to maintain that same water level. Place in a sunny spot, a south window, and germination should occur anywhere from two weeks to three months.

As you can see, patience is required here, but once germination takes place, things happen fast. Roots are sent down into the jar while a sprout shoots up above. At that time, the first true leaves will appear.

This can be an interesting experience to watch if you have any small children around the house. They can see right into the glass jar.

When roots fill the jar, transplant into a six-inch pot filled with regular potting soil. Always keep the soil moist and never let it dry out. Otherwise, the tips of the plant's leaves will turn brown. They'll get stiff and crinkly.

While the plant is still in the jar, do not fertilize. The plant is able to feed upon the reserve food which is stored in the pit.

Once transplanting has taken place, however, and the seedling has had time in which to adjust to its new environment, say six weeks to three months, feed every month with a water soluble fertilizer.

There is still another method in which to start the avocado pit growing, and that is right in the pot, itself. To do this, start the same way as with the jar method, that is, by thoroughly cleaning the pit.

Then select a pot that is six or eight inches in diameter and six to ten inches deep. See to it that there is adequate drainage. Then fill the container with sand, sterilized garden soil, or a regular potting mix.

Plant the pit with its pointed end facing up, covering

just half of it with the soil. If you wish to speed the germination process, remove the outer coat of the pit. Or, cut off the top half inch of the pointed end.

Place the pot in a warm spot in your home. Give it plenty of light and water. Germination should occur in approximately four weeks.

Wait a few months before fertilizing, still using one of the water soluble plant foods.

When the plant outgrows its container, transplant into a larger one, the next size up in pot diameter. Keep pinching back so that the plant doesn't become too tall and look scraggly. Pinching back makes the plant more bushy.

You probably won't get fruit but you'll get a beautiful foliage plant.

And that's nice, isn't it?

# THE COCONUT

This chapter, like the banana, is quite unique as we continue with *cocos nucifera*—the coconut!

According to Naturalist Eileen Greason of the Essex County Park Commission's Center for Environmental Studies in Roseland, New Jersey, special patience is required here as germination for the coconut palm can take anywhere from two months to *one year* to germinate.

Extraordinary, isn't it?

The coconut, as you may already know, is a fruit that grows on a tall tree in tropical climates. One tree can produce as many as one hundred coconuts in a single year.

The coconut has a smooth, hard outer shell but when we buy it in the supermarket, it has been removed, leaving the inner part of the fruit with its fibrous husk.

This is really the seed part of the coconut. It consists of a white, sweet-tasting meat. It is probably the largest kind of seed there is.

And it is an unusual one at that, because while most other seeds store a simple supply of condensed food for the new plant, the coconut houses a nourishing liquid that is referred to as "coconut milk."

If the coconut falls into the sea, it has the capacity to float. Its thick husk protects the seed from the salt water and impact of the waves.

When the coconut reaches land, the food and liquid that is stored within helps the new plant to begin to grow and take root in the soil. The new seedling will then grow out of the coconut through one of the three eyes in its shell.

But let's get started now, and begin our own coconut palm tree. Maybe you will and maybe you won't get coconuts, but this project is, in itself, adventurous. Promise, though, to be patient.

Remember, when you buy a coconut, you're going to get it without its original outer shell. This means, of course, that we're going to work with the rough, fibrous part.

Taking this fact into consideration, soak the coconut, as is, in a bucket of lukewarm water for one week. The purpose of this procedure is to make the coconut think it is in the ocean. Quite a bit of psychology attached to this, isn't there? I hate to say "I told you so," but didn't I tell you that this was going to be a unique project?

At the end of one week, place the coconut onto a tray of sand. The purpose of this procedure is to make the coconut think it has landed on the beach after a week of tossing around in that bucket of ocean.

Tilt it at about a forty-five degree angle with its eyes facing upward. That is the end that must be kept constantly moist. It is the coconut's soft area. Squeeze it. You can feel how much water it has absorbed from all that soaking.

Here comes the part where patience is needed, the part where you'll have to play a waiting game until germination occurs. When it finally does, however, the coconut will get a crack in its shell. The sprout will shoot up through it.

At this point, find a large enough container in which

to pot the coconut. Fill it with regular potting soil and plant the coconut, leaving it at the same angle that you previously had it. Make sure that half the coconut is exposed above the soil.

The young seedling will get feathery green leaves. As growth progresses, pinch off any unhealthy-looking ones for they can only rob the tree of its growing strength.

The palm, remember, is a tropical inhabitant, so give it plenty of sun. Since it likes warmth, too, try to keep it in the warmest spot in your home.

Feed with one of the water soluble fertilizers, following the manufacturer's instructions. Fish emulsion is preferable. Keep the soil constantly moist, never soggy or roots can rot; never too dry, either.

As you can see, there's nothing complicated about starting the coconut palm tree. The main thing is the waiting. But the expression "The best things are worth waiting for" is very applicable here.

Right?

# PART 3: NUTS

# THE ALMOND

Originally, almonds came from Mediterranean countries. However, practically all almonds grown here in the United States come from California.

The almond grows on a tree of medium height that is related to the peach. When the tree is in bloom, beautiful pinkish-white blossoms similar to that of the peach appear. They open in the early part of spring long before the appearance of the tree's long, pointed leaves.

A tan-colored, hard outer shell houses the edible kernel with which we are all familiar. The nuts are delicious when eaten whole, but are equally good when put into candies or cakes.

Almonds contain a large amount of oil. In bitter almonds, as opposed to the sweet variety, there is a poisonous substance known as prussic acid. Once this poison is removed, the oil is safe and is used as a flavoring extract.

In order to grow an almond tree, do not use almonds that have been roasted or salted. You must buy the unprocessed kind from the health food store.

Since almonds come from cool regions, you may, if you wish, place them into a plastic bag along with some moistened milled sphagnum moss and refrigerate in or out of their shells for about six weeks. I might mention, however, that the Essex County Park Commission's Center for Environmental Studies in Roseland, New Jersey, achieved success in growing the almond minus the refrigeration process.

In any event, because of the almond's large root system, select a deep container with which to start, transplanting later to an even larger size. Fill with regular potting soil and place a nicked almond about an inch deep. Cover with a thin layer of the mixture.

Germination takes two to three weeks. During this time, provide good bottom heat by placing the container on top of the refrigerator or other electrical appliance. Do not let the soil dry out. Keep it constantly moist.

When the plant is actively growing, keep in a south window but watch that the leaves don't burn from a too-hot sun.

This plant grows extremely fast. By the time four months go by, it will already be about two feet tall. Leaves are attractive and have serated edges.

One day the almond will turn into a beautiful standing plant. Keep pinching back so that it looks nice and full.

Feed with fish emulsion according to the manufacturer's instructions.

# THE PEANUT

The peanut originated in South America. Eventually, Old World navigators and explorers introduced it to Africa and Europe. At one time, peanuts were used aboard ship as the main diet to feed slaves.

In the 1800s, George Washington Carver, a black American who became famous for his research in agriculture, conducted endless experiments with the peanut. He made about three hundred products in his laboratory ranging from instant coffee to soap to ink.

Another interesting item about peanuts lies in the fact that jars of peanut seeds were discovered in ancient graves in Peru.

Furthermore, Indians in Virginia were already raising peanuts by the time the settlers arrived. In fact, peanuts were the first gift that Indians gave to white men.

During colonial times, colonists used to plant peanuts along with artichokes for their pigs to eat. Then, when hams were cooked, this peanut/artichoke diet gave the meat a superlative flavor.

Today, peanuts are grown along the East Coast from Virginia to Florida. They are also grown along the Gulf Coast to Texas and in all adjoining inland States.

And of course, former President Carter was, himself, a peanut grower. As you would expect, the popularity of the peanut rose when he was elected.

Surprisingly, the peanut is not really a nut. It is actually the fruit of a legume or pod and is related to the pea and the bean. It is also referred to as the goober nut, the goober pea, and just plain goober.

The peanut is quite valuable. It is an excellent source of Vitamins A and B. And of course, next to the hamburger, peanut butter is one of America's most favorite foods.

From the peanut, oil is extracted to make salad oils, margarine, and vegetable shortening. It is also used for packing fish.

In addition, peanut oil is used in making shampoos, shaving creams, nitro-glycerin for explosives, soap, face powder, and even glue.

Also, when peanut roots are left in the soil, it enriches the soil with nitrogen.

To plant peanuts, you must use the raw kind, that is, unprocessed peanuts. Do not use any that have been roasted or salted. Your best bet is to purchase them at your local health food store.

Then, select a four-inch container and fill it with a regular potting mixture. Remove the shells from three peanuts. Positioning them on their side, place directly into the soil, covering the peanuts with a thin layer of the mixture. Water lightly and keep in a warm location.

The peanut germinates in about one week. At first you will see a loop-shaped sprout which is called the hypercotyl arch. As this straightens up, poking its way up through the top of the soil, cotyledons will appear, the first true leaves.

Because the growing process of the peanut is so unique, perhaps you might consider growing the peanuts in a glass container so that small children could look in and watch the event.

As growth continues, the peanut will grow into an upright plant. Once it gets to be about twelve inches tall, transplant into a ten-inch pot. Remember to keep the soil constantly moist.

Later, a pretty yellow flower will develop above the soil. It is able to pollinate itself and once it does, it sends shoots below the surface of the soil. That's where the peanuts form.

Once the peanuts begin to set, the plant starts to die back. You can either dig the peanuts up and eat them or just leave them in the soil where they will sprout again.

Remember to always keep the soil moist and give the plant a southern exposure. Use any commercial fertilizer, but in the beginning, use at half strength. Build slowly up to full strength.

# SUNFLOWERS

Yes, this is a seedy subject, indeed, as we continue with sunflower seeds. You probably have some in your home right now, if you love them as much as I do.

Did you ever stop to think about where sunflower seeds come from? We are so used to buying them conveniently bagged for us. Nothing to do but crack them open and pop a handful of those tasty morsels into our mouths.

My own father loves them so much that he buys them by the pound. So many empty shells are piled up that when he goes to empty them, the sound they make as they cascade into the brown paper bag sounds like a thunderstorm.

We get sunflower seeds from the flower it is named after—the sunflower. And a very befitting name it is, too, because the flower, with its large yellow head surrounded by rays of petals, does, in fact, resemble the sun.

The annual garden variety, the kind we are talking about here, is very popular compared to other species of its kind.

To plant sunflower seeds, buy the unprocessed ones that can be bought in the health food store. Do not use any that have been roasted and salted. They won't grow.

The sunflower, which is supported by a rough, hairy stem is going to grow extremely tall, so although you can start it in the house, it will eventually have to be transferred outside. A good time to start the seeds is in the spring, around April.

To begin, soak the *unshelled* seeds overnight. They'll crack open faster this way. Next morning, select a four-inch container and fill with regular potting soil.

Place three seeds about an inch and a half deep, covering them with a thin layer of the mixture. Water lightly and keep in a south window. Germination will occur within two weeks.

Keep transplanting into larger pots for as long as you can, fertilizing with any house plant food, following the manufacturer's instructions. However, when you see that the plant is growing too large to keep indoors, transfer to the outside. It takes four months for the plant to become a giant sunflower.

The plant will form little yellow petals around its flower, and there, seeds make a spiral pattern around its center. Although it depends upon the size of the flower, it can yield as many as one hundred seeds.

Keep soil constantly moist.

An important thing for you to remember is that by placing the plant outside, it can attract garden insects. Therefore, use an organic pesticide such as rotenone.

# PART 4: VEGETABLES

# GARLIC

Believe it or not, this strongly flavored plant belongs to the lily family. Except, unlike the lily, the garlic plant is a bulb that can be divided into cloves and eaten.

As you well know, garlic must be eaten sparingly. Otherwise, you can literally reek from its powerful odor. However, if it is used in porper proportions, it is a real flavor booster in meats and vegtables.

And what about that extra touch it gives to salads and pickles? Ever try garlic butter on French bread? Such deliciousness cannot be denied.

Pertaining to garlic, did you know that . . .

. . . it was used as far back as Biblical times?

. . . it was once worn around the neck to keep evil and sickness away?

. . . in movie films, garlic was worn around the neck by a would-be victim to ward off an attack by a vampire?

. . . it is used as a bug repellent in the garden?

. . . if you chew a sprig of fresh parsley after eating garlic-flavored food, your breath will be freshened!

Many people are under the impression that if you try to grow a plant from the garlic itself, the plant will have a disagreeable odor. Not true.

So the next time you're puttering around the kitchen, save one of the cloves from the garlic bulb. Make certain the papery covering around it has been removed before it is planted. And be careful not to nick the clove with a sharp fingernail to ensure the absence of that unwanted unpleasant scent.

Then select a pot with adequate drainage and fill it with an all-purpose potting mixture. Place the clove so that its pointed end is showing just above the soil. Germination will occur within ten days.

Keep the soil constantly moist and supply as much sunlight as possible so that the plant won't become scraggly.

The garlic grows very fast. By the time the plant is one month old, it will already be a foot tall.

Feed with full strength fish emulsion every two weeks.

As growth continues, the garlic plant will develop a flower—a purple cluster on a long stem.

Will wonders never cease?

# BEETS

Remember that pretty purple plant in Grandma's kitchen? Now how about one in yours?

You know, originally, the beet plant grew wild near the Caspian Sea. It was used as food during ancient times as well as by the Spaniards around the fifteenth century.

They must have known even then that the top of the beet, referred to as beet greens, is a rich source of vitamins and minerals. In fact, they are even healthier than the root itself. Next time you are pickling beets, see what you can whip up with the greens, too.

Let me give you fair warning, though, because you are in for quite a surprise. The beet is going to turn into a beautiful bushy house plant. It will last for about two years. After that, it will die back and you'll have to plant a new one. But it's easy.

If you purchase a beet that has no greens on it, fine. If you should buy one with the greens still attached, remove them. Most likely they'll be scraggly and unattractive from just lying around. Otherwise, if any "nice" foliage is present, keep it. This can give you something of a headstart.

Thoroughly scrub the beet with a vegtable brush under warm running water. This procedure helps to step up the sprouting stage. Then fill an eight-inch container with regular potting soil.

Set the beet into the mixture so that the pointed end is face down. With it properly positioned, leave about a quarter of the beet exposed above the soil's surface.

As growth progresses, lovely green leaves will appear, each one having a pretty purpley-red vertical stripe or vein going down its center.

Eventually, the beet will grow sideshoots. Pinch them off. Periodically pinch off dead leaves, too. During the summer, the beet might get a white, spike-like flower, but pinch it off because it somehow weakens the plant. Besides, the leaves are beautiful enough all by themselves.

Keep in a southern window and maintain a regular watering schedule. Soil should be constantly moist, never soggy or overly dry.

Feed with one of the water soluble fertilizers once a month, and follow the manufacturer's instructions.

There is a possibility that you could run into an aphid problem with this plant. Should this occur, remove insects with an organic spray such as rotenone.

# LENTILS

This is the first food plant ever to be grown by Man. And no wonder, for lentils rate high in nutrition. They are rich in carbohydrates and protein.

Lentils, as you may already know, belong to the pea and bean family. They are cultivated in southern Europe, Egypt, and Western Asia. Now it is popularly raised here in the United States as one of America's most favorite foods.

The lentil is shaped like a lens. A point of interest lies in the fact that the lens was so-named because of its striking resemblance to this seed.

The lentil makes a beautiful annual house plant. You'll periodically have to start new ones but the task is a simple one for lentils germinate quickly.

To begin, soak four or five lentils overnight at room temperature. Next morning, fill a four-inch container with dampened milled sphagnum moss and place your seeds. Germination takes place in about ten days.

At that time, fill an eight-inch container with an all-purpose potting mixture into which you will set your seedlings. Water on a regular basis and always keep the soil constantly moist. If you don't, the plant can wither and die.

This is a sun-loving plant, so set it in a southern exposure. Feed with a water soluble fertilizer according to the manufacturer's directions.

As growth progresses, check that the plant doesn't become potbound. Make sure there are no roots showing through the drainage hole.

Note that in a series of repottings, you should end up with a little over a ten-inch container.

The plant is going to develop attractive compound leaves, each leaf having a tendril growing from its tip. You can train these vines to grow up a trellis or you may keep it as a hanging plant in your kitchen.

Later, expect small white flowers to develop. They are going to throw out seeds with which to set pods. If you wish, pinch them back to prevent this from happening.

Otherwise, let Nature take its course and let the pods set. At this time, the plant will begin to die back. Just collect your seeds and grow a new one. There's no reason why you can't keep 'em comin'.

# PEAS

Although the exact origin of peas is somewhat clouded, it is thought that peas originated either in Eastern Europe or Western Asia.

However, it *is* known that peas were widely used in prehistoric times. Attempts were made to trace back to the stone age and dried seeds were discovered lying among relics of the Swiss Lake and in scattered villages.

The Chinese grew and ate peas in 2000 B.C. and the Bible mentions it, too, among its ancient pages. Still, the consumption of peas wasn't really referred to with any great gusto until 1066—the time of the Norman conquest.

Peas were first introduced to America around the 1800s, and today, with canning and freezing processes in use, they are widely used.

When you are dining out, notice that the restaurant's menu lists peas with great dignity and elegance, for the vegetable isn't merely referred to by its common name, but as "legumes."

Interestingly, to differentiate common garden peas from the dried or split kind, peas are quite often called green peas, or English peas.

The vegetable grows in a vining pattern on low-growing bushes. They progress very rapidly and in farming, is an important cool-weather crop.

To get peas at their peak, that is, when they are the most delicious, they must be picked just as the seeds mature in the pod.

Otherwise, if you wait until they become fully ripe, the pods shrivel up and the seeds turn into tiny, dry, wrinkled pellets. In fact, that is how you get dried peas, by simply leaving them on the vine for a greater length of time.

Did you also know that . . .

. . . one pound of dry peas has 1,655 calories?

. . . one pound of succulent green peas has 465 calories?

. . . peas have almost as much protein and energy value that meat has, and that they are an excellent source of vitamins A and D?

. . . the peas can be turned into attractive house plants and that is what we are going to do right now?

But first, before we get started, are you going to use fresh or dry peas? If you are going to use the fresh kind, just take them out of the pod and place them into a regular potting mixture.

Otherwise, if you intend to use the dry peas, make sure you soak them overnight. Next morning, place five into a six-inch container that has been filled with a good all-purpose potting composition. Lay them an inch-and-a-half deep and cover with the soil. Water lightly.

Remember—peas are fast growers. Germination takes place within two weeks. When it does, maintain a regular watering routine, keeping the soil constantly moist, watering only when it begins to dry out.

When the plant is actively growing, it will become viny. Little tendrils will appear. They'll want to creep onto something, so train them onto a trellis.

Peas are self-pollinating and later on, they develop

small, white flowers and set their pods. Keep in a cool place, on an east or west window during the summer. There it will receive good air circulation from breezes wafting into the house. In the winter, keep in a south window.

In feeding, use one of the water soluble fertilizers about every two or three weeks. Follow the manufacturer's instructions for best results.

This plant is an annual, that is, it is short-lived. You must start a new one every year.

But it's easy, isn't it?

# THE SWEET POTATO

Remember the sweet potato your science teacher once grew? Chances were that he didn't interest you then while you waited impatiently for the school bell to ring. What mattered most at the time was three o'clock, time to go home.

However, maybe that teacher really knew what he was talking about, for the sweet potato, an annual vine, can be turned into a very attractive plant. And believe it or not, it is related to the morning-glory.

The sweet potato rates high in nurtrition. It provides a rich source of vitamins A and C. In addition, it provides nearly five percent of the protein that is required by the adult male as well as six percent calcium, nine percent phosphorous, eleven percent iron, ten percent thiamin, five percent niacin, and almost six percent riboflavin. With all these available nutrients, a sweet potato that is five inches long and two inches in diameter yields about one hundred seventy calories.

Historically speaking, ancient Mayan and Peruvian civilizations grew and cultivated this vegetable. And so did the primitive inhabitants of the South Pacific Islands for they used the sweet potato as an important part of many important rituals.

Christopher Columbus, on his fourth voyage to the West Indian nations, noticed even then, that people were raising this edible tuber. As early as 1648, colonists who settled in Virginia grew the sweet potato from roots they obtained in the West Indies.

Let us get started now and get this plant growing. To begin, select a large potato and with a vegetable brush, scrub it thoroughly under warm running water. This step is important in case the potato has been treated to prevent sprouting.

According to the Essex County Park Commission's Center for Environmental Studies in Roseland, New Jersey, it is best to use a clay pot for this project because clay will protect the sweet potato from rotting.

Fill this container with an all-purpose potting mixture. Then set the tuber in, about half way, with its pointed end down. Water when the top half inch of soil becomes dry.

Or, thoroughly scrub a large sweet potato. Insert three to four toothpicks into its middle. Suspend the vegetable in a jar of water so that the bottom half is submerged. Always keep the water fresh to prevent rotting.

Within a month, the potato will form many white roots. You may continue to grow it in water or you can pot it. Potting, however, extends the life of the plant by several months.

When repotting, choose a large enough container to accommodate the entire potato. Then cover with two-thirds to three-quarters soil.

Later, your plant will develop greenish-purple leaves and long vines, perfect for a sunny window box. In the fall, when you clean out the window box to bring the plant indoors, there'll be plenty of sweet potatoes on the bottom.

You may prune this plant to make it bush out. New

plants can be started from the cuttings when placed into a jar of water. There, they'll take root. Just pot them and you have made additional plants.

When keeping this plant indoors, place it in a sunny spot. Feed with any plant food following the manufacture's instructions.

# LIMA BEANS

Lima beans are natives of the Western Hemisphere. It is believed that they originated in Central America. The smaller variety has been cultivated since prehistoric times in North America, but the larger variety was developed in South America. Especially in Peru. In fact, that is how Lima became the capital city of that country.

Lima beans have great nutritional value as they are high in thiamine, riboflavin, phosphorus, and iron. They are also a good source of protein.

Like many other types of beans, limas are really seeds which grow inside pods. They can be grown on vines while others can grow on a bush. Still, there are others that can be trained up a trellis or a pole.

As you can see, lima beans are very accommodating. They'll grow just about any which way. They are exceptionally easy to germinate. That is why this is something that the children, as well as yourself, will enjoy doing.

However, before we get started, let me ask you a question. Are you going to use dry beans? If your answer is yes, then first place your beans into a strainer and rinse them under warm running water. Let them soak overnight, too. Next morning, simply set them directly into an all-purpose potting mixture.

On the other hand, if you're using fresh beans, select a wide-mouthed jar. Soak some blotting paper or paper toweling and mold it to the inside of the jar. It should conform perfectly with the jar when you are through.

Now place the lima beans in between the glass and the blotter. The blotter must be kept constantly moist, so fill the jar with a quarter of an inch of water.

Germination will occur within a week and you will be able to watch the event through the glass. As germination takes place, roots are sent down into the jar, while up above, cotyledons, the first leaves, make their appearance.

At this time, very, very carefully peel away the blotting paper. And just as carefully, remove the fragile sprouts. Place them into a container that has been filled with regular potting soil, setting them in an inch-and-a-half to two inches deep. Maintain a regular watering schedule, keeping the soil constantly moist. Feed with fish emulsion according to the formulator's directions.

The lima bean truly makes a beautiful plant. It develops attractive large leaves with flowers that grow in the shape of a spike. The whole plant bears a striking resemblance to the philodendron.

These flowers take about a month to appear. At that time, they'll produce new pods that you can either pluck off and eat—or plant.

If you wish, place three plants into a pretty ten-inch pot to use as a hanging basket. Or, train the vines to grow up a trellis. However, if you desire a nice bushy plant, keep pinching back until the effect you want is achieved.

This plant loves the sun so keep it in a south window.

Okay?

# TURNIPS

Turnips, once a common food of the Greeks and the Romans, have been a favorite food in England and in northern Europe for a very long time. They have been grown in the United States dating back to the early 1700s.

Today, turnips are grown mostly in the United States, Canada, and parts of Europe. They grow very easily and readily adapt to home gardens.

Turnips are great for dieting because they are so low in calories. They're a good source of vitamins A, B, and C, too.

Actually, this vegetable belongs to the mustard branch of the cabbage family. It has a distinctive yet bland flavor and can be eaten either raw or cooked. Although the large, upper portion of the root is usually what's eaten, the greens can be equally utilized.

The turnip makes a nice plant when green leaves contrast against its purple top. It will last for as long as two years, when you'll have to start another plant. But come. Let us now begin.

Remove any unsightly leaves from the turnip, but keep the nice ones. Then, scrub it thoroughly with a vegetable brush under warm running water.

Cleaning it this way helps to speed up sprouting. After the cleansing procedure has been carried out, select a container with adequate drainage. An eight incher would be fine. Fill it with a regular potting mix.

Position the turnip so that its pointed end is facing downward. In this manner, place it into the soil. Be sure to leave about a quarter of the turnip exposed above the surface of the soil.

As growth progresses, pretty curly leaves will appear. Later, yellow flowers.

You'll get some sideshoots, too. Pinch them off, otherwise they'll weaken the plant. Every once in awhile look for dead leaves and pinch them off so that they won't weaken the plant, either.

There is a chance that the turnip plant could get aphids. If that happens, destroy the pests with an organic spray. Rotenone is desirable.

Maintain a regular watering routine, watering when you notice that the soil is beginning to dry out.

This plant requires plenty of sun so keep in a south window.

Feed with a water soluble fertilizer every month and follow the manufacturer's directions.

If you wish, you can select an attractive bowl and add a layer of pebbles to it. Place either a whole small turnip on the pebbles, or a larger one that has been cut in half, its cut side facing down. Add more pebbles, leaving an inch or two of the turnip exposed. Fill with water no higher than the level of the pebbles. Do not let the water dry out.

# SOYBEANS

Soybeans made their first appearance as a cultivated crop in northern China about three thousand years ago. The ancient Chinese considered the soybean as one of the five most important grains needed for living. In 2838 B.C., the Emperor Shung Nung wrote a description of the plant and this is said to be the earliest recording of the soybean.

Soybeans were first introduced to Europe around the 1600s and not until the early 1800s did they catch on in America. It wasn't until the vicinity of World War II that soybeans made their mark as an important agricultural crop.

Besides the United States, soybean growers include China, Manchuria, Korea, Japan, and Indonesia. However, soybeans are also grown in other parts of the world such as Brazil, India, the Philippines, Russia, Czechoslovakia, South Africa, Canada, New Zealand, and many other places.

Soybeans have self-pollinating flowers that can be purple or white. Slightly curved and hairy pods contain between three to five beans.

When soybeans are eaten as green beans, they are much easier to shell if the pods are plunged into boiling water for about two minutes. However, when dry mature soybeans are desired, plants are cut when the pods are turning brown.

Soybeans are very easy to sprout. In preparation, soak them overnight, then place into a wide-mouthed jar that is large enough for the beans to swell at least six times their original bulk as they sprout. Cover with cheesecloth, securing it tightly with a rubber band.

The next day, drain off the water and lay the jar on its side in a warm dark place. Keep adding water, as many as two to three times a day. Shake the jar to rinse the seeds. Drain well. Place the jar back on its side.

A word of caution here; do not let the seeds sit in water for too long a time. Neither should you neglect them so that they dry out. Both of these no-no's can ruin the beans.

Germination occurs in three to five days. The sprouts are fully grown and ready to use when they are two to three inches long. At the time of germination, place the jar on a sunny windowsill so that the sprouts can turn green. Once you harvest them, keep in a cool place.

Otherwise, grow the beans in regular potting soil. Give them plenty of sun, water, and feed with one of the commercial plant foods according to the manufacturer's directions, and—poof!—you've got yourself a pretty hanging plant.

# GARBANZO BEANS

In contrast to the coconut, let's concern ourselves, now, with something that requires practically no waiting at all for germination to take place. Thus, operation garbanzo beans!

Because garbanzo beans are so easy to get growing, you might like to have the children participate. What better way is there to keep them occupied one stay-in type of day?

One day, when the weather report predicts showers for the following day, the morning before, have the children prepare the beans. Give them a vessel in which to soak the beans in warm water overnight. If you have three children, give them each two beans. Two children, give them three apiece. As you can see, we are using six garbanzo beans.

After they have been soaked, dry the beans by rolling them in paper toweling. Then fill a container with moistened milled sphagnum moss and set the beans in about a half an inch deep.

Germination will occur within a week to ten days. When it does, select three of the healthiest sprouts and place them in a four-inch pot that has been filled with a regular potting mixture. Cover with half an inch of soil and water lightly.

Garbanzo beans have a pretty expansive root system so keep your eyes on the drainage holes for signs of transplanting. Keep repotting until the plant ends up in a ten incher. It could take three months for the plant to reach this stage.

There will be many compound leaves that have tendrils. You can either train them to climb up a trellis or grow the plant in a hanging planter.

Keep the soil constantly moist and never let it dry out. Place in a south window and feed every two weeks with fish emulsion, following the manufacturer's instructions.

This plant is an annual. Eventually, tiny white flowers that resemble the sweet pea will appear. Once they fall off, seed pods grow and swell. Then they'll turn brown at which time you can pluck them off the vine and put them where they can dry out.

The pod can be easily peeled off. You can either plant the beans again to form new plants or you can eat them. Why don't you let the children decide?

It is, after all, their project!

# THE LOVE APPLE

Of course, we are talking about the tomato. How did the tomato earn its nickname? Well, it goes something like this...

Long before the arrival of Christopher Columbus, the tomato had already gained some popularity in North and South America. Seeds of the tomato were then sent to Europe where they were raised in private gardens. For decorative purposes, mainly. Somehow, as the story goes, a superstition soon developed that the tomato inspired orgiastic lust in the breast of Man. Thus, the nickname, "love apple."

Later, the early colonists brought tomato seeds into Virginia. In the beginning, they, too, grew the plant among ornamental flowers in private gardens. Finally, Thomas Jefferson, one of the first Americans to do so, ventured forth to eat the tomato. However, even then, most people didn't eat it until the early 1800s.

The tomato is rich in vitamins A and C. Its versatility makes it an important and popular food item for it can be eaten raw, broiled, stewed, and almost any-which-way you want to cook it. Dieters, in particular, make excellent use of the tomato's low-calorie content.

But now, how would you like to have a nice tomato plant? It can be done, you know. And although its's an annual, lasting approximately four months, a new one can always be started with ease.

You can plant tomato seeds any time of the year. However, for best results, because tomatoes are true lovers of sunshine, it would be ideal to start them in the late spring.

That is, unless you are going to use the seeds from a hybrid. Those can be grown any time at all, even in the winter since they don't require a bright hot sun. These grow about two feet tall.

In addition, tomato seeds can be grown in a hanging planter or in a large pot. They don't take too well to transplanting, so use a ten incher right from the start.

To begin, remove the seeds from the tomato. Place in a closely-meshed strainer (you don't want the seeds to fall through too large an opening) and rinse under warm running water. Dry by rolling the seeds in between sheets of paper toweling.

Then, fill a container with a regular potting mixture. Place five seeds, and water lightly. Germination can occur anywhere between two to two-and-a-half weeks.

As growth progresses, remove the weaker sprouts, trying to end up with three good healthy plants.

Eventually, a pretty yellow, bell-shaped flower will appear. As its base begins to swell, a green tomato will appear. After it has been picked, the plant's strength begins to ebb until about four months later, its growing cycle ceases entirely. Time to begin a new tomato plant.

To take care of the plant while it is in its prime, adopt a regular watering routine, making sure that the soil is kept constantly moist. Keep where full sun can get at it and feed with tomato food according to the manufacturer's directions.

# THE CARROT

Did you know that carrots were used by the Ancient Greeks and Romans? Yes, it's true. But they didn't use it for food. They used it as medicine. And early settlers in Virginia and Massachussetts raised carrots. Ate 'em, too.

The carrot actually belongs to the parsley family. It's very hardy because it can live in the winter time, providing the weather isn't extreme. On the other hand, it is also strong enough to withstand the heat of summer.

Carrots are rich in sugar. They also are high in iron content, vitamins A and B1 and have smaller amounts of vitamins C and B2.

Believe it or not, the carrot is a potential plant. And an attractive one at that, too. Use one or several in order to obtain a nice full effect. Eileen Greason, greenhouse keeper with the Essex County Park Commission's Center for Environmental Studies in Roseland, New Jersey, has grown as many as three in a six-inch container.

If you've purchased fresh carrots with their green tops still attached, cut them off because they're unattractive and scraggly. However, if you've purchased the clean and prepackaged ones, their greenery has already been detached and you can start the plant from scratch.

To begin, scrub the carrot thoroughly with a vegetable brush under warm running water. Preparing it thusly opens it up, makes the carrot more viable so that it will be more susceptible for quicker sprouting.

Next, chop off the top so that two inches of the carrot remains. Then select a four-inch container if you are planting one carrot, larger, if you are planting many. Check for adequate drainage, then fill with a regular potting mixture.

With the cut side facing down, place the carrot so that a quarter of an inch is exposed above the soil's surface. Do not pack the soil too compactly.

Maintain a regular watering routine, keeping the soil constantly moist. Never let it dry out completely. Don't overwater either because a soggy condition can cause rotting.

Place in a south window for this plant loves sun. Every two weeks feed with any plant food, following manufacturer's instructions.

If you wish, select an attractive bowl and add a layer of pebbles. Place three carrots, cut side down, onto this arrangement. Carefully add another layer of pebbles, just enough to leave an inch or two of the carrots exposed. Fill with water, not going over the level of the pebbles.

You will find, that as growth progresses, the carrot is going to develop pretty green feathery foliage. Later, a lovely green composite flower will appear. Much to one's delight, it strongly resembles Queen Anne's Lace, a lovely flower that can be seen growing all over the countryside.

Isn't that nice?

# SQUASH

Actually, squash is a relative of the pumpkin family and it is no wonder that the history of each runs into one another. Both, you see, originated from tropical America.

In fact, squash was raised on the Atlantic Coast way before Christopher Columbus discovered America. Later, however, squash was introduced to European countries such as England and France.

Squash does very well as a summer crop in France. There, it is called *la gourde*. In England, fall and winter squash don't adjust properly to the country's climate.

Squash, a viny plant, is a warm-weather crop. A fast grower, too. There are many different existing varieties. The giant yellow crookneck, for example, has a strange appearance, indeed, with its long curved swan-like neck and wart-like complexion. To look at it, you would never think that inside, the meat is a pretty cream color and quite smooth in texture.

In addition to the crookneck is another odd-featured squash named white bush. This is a summer favorite among the crowd because of its peculiar shape, rather star-like. Sometimes it is even called "scalloped" or "pattypan."

Butternut squash, which in a way resembles a giant light bulb, has firm orange-colored meat. This, too, is a popular variety because of its pleasing sweet taste.

Sounding, and maybe looking a little like Old Mother Hubbard, is the Hubbard squash. This is just about the most popular of the winter species. It can grow quite large and has rather a rich, dryish flesh.

Nutritionally speaking, squashes have a certain amount of energy-giving value. They, particularly the yellow-fleshed winter variety, are rich in vitamin A.

Squash can be divided into three categories. Summer, autumn, and winter. Summer squashes are harvested while they are at the immature stage. The autumn variety can be picked when they are almost mature and may be stored for a few months at a time. However, if stored too long, there is a loss of flavor. With winter varieties, the story is a little different for squash is harvested just at the peak of maturity. These have hard outer shells and may be stored for any length of time.

But surely you must realize by now, for we've covered so much ground already, that you can take the seeds of the squash and grow them into an attractive house plant. Although this is an annual, lasting only a few months, at least you will have had some pleasure with its short-lived presence. Just grow a new one to take place. Now that you've become a pro—it's easy

To begin, remove the seeds from the squash. They'll be flat and most likely, will have pulp adhering to them. Therefore, place the seeds in a closely-meshed strainer and rinse them thoroughly under warm running water. Make sure you get all that pulp off, because once it starts to rot, it will cause the seeds to decay.

Then, you may either let the seeds dry out overnight or plant immediately into regular potting soil. Since they don't take transplanting well, select a large container as the plant's permanent home.

In the pot, make a mound with the soil and set three seeds, about an inch deep. Water lightly and keep in a warm spot. Germination takes about one week to ten days. Remember, the squash is a fast grower.

The plant will develop rather large leaves, three to four inches in width. On the base of each leaf is a tendril that you can train to grow up a trellis—or just use the plant as a hanging plant in your kitchen.

About two months later the plant is going to develop pretty yellow bell-shaped flowers. Outdoors, bees do the pollinating, but inside, in order to get the plant to fruit, you'll have to pollinate it yourself by dabbing at each flower with a soft brush.

This is a sun-loving plant so provide a south exposure. Maintain a regular watering schedule, keeping the soil constantly moist. Don't let it become drenched or the plant's roots can rot.

Feed with a water soluble fertilizer about every two weeks following the manufacturer's directions.

Should insect problems occur use an organic spray such as rotenone.

# THE RADISH

I know, you probably never thought you'd be growing a radish as a house plant, at least not until you
picked up this book. But yes, it can be done. As a
matter of fact, they are so easy to grow, that I, myself,
grew too many and gave most of them away. To my
friends, of course.

We are so used to seeing radishes in the supermarket
that we never give them a second thought as to where
they might have come from. Well, radishes are nothing
new in that they were grown long before you and I
ever thought of them as house plants. Interestingly,
they were raised in China hundreds and hundreds of
years ago.

The radish belongs to the mustard family. Besides
being a popular crop in the United States, it is also
grown in Europe, North America, and Asia. While it is
true that the radish leaves something to be desired in
the way of nutritional value, it *does* add zest and zing to
salads. It is also popularly used as a garnish, to dress up
various food preparations.

In all actuality, the radish is really a cluster of mus-
tard-like leaves growing on top of a root. However, it is
the root portion that we eat and refer to as the "radish."

This is an annual plant, living just a few months, but
it is a fast grower and new plants can be started at a
moment's notice. There are all kinds of radishes, too.
Red, white, spring, and winter. Among radish varieties
is a giant beet-shaped monster known as Sakurajimi.
Sounding more like the name of a science-fiction

movie, this species can grow up to fifty pounds and more. Will wonders never cease?

Although the radish can withstand frost, it is tempermental in that it cannot take heat well. In fact, a particular type of radish that farmers grow has to be planted in the fall, about seventy-five days before the onset of frost. When harvested, it can be stored during the winter just like the turnip.

Now that we've gotten acquainted with the radish, how about growing one into a house plant? If you purchase ones that come straight from the farm, all the leaves will be intact. Snip them off and start over because they are unattractive. Too long and too scraggly.

Start with a good firm radish, not one that is old and molding in the refrigerator. You need a radish that is easy to sprout, one that is viable.

Wash the radish gently under warm running water. If you wish, you may prepare three to place in a six-inch container. Pat dry with paper toweling and place, root side down, into a regular potting mixture. Leave a portion of the radish showing above the surface of the soil. Water lightly.

Germination occurs almost immediately. What you'll get are attractive curly green leaves. Later, the plant will develop a spike-like flower.

If you wish, you can also grow radishes by arranging them in a pretty shallow bowl. Set them with their root side facing down on a layer of pebbles. Carefully, so as not to bruise the radishes, add additional pebbles to keep them stationary.

Next, fill the bowl with water, but only enough to

touch the level of the pebbles. Maintain the water level in this fashion from thereon in, adding more water when necessary.

To maintain the plant in potting soil, however, water on a regular basis but don't allow the soil to become soggy. If you do, the radish can rot. Also, give the plant good light. Put it in a south or west window. If the sun becomes too hot either remove the plant to a cooler, more shaded area, or draw the curtains as protection.

Feed every week with one of the plant foods out on the market, following the manufacturer's directions. This might prolong the life of the plant but due to the nature of things, it is, in all reality, a short-lived species, and will have to be replaced.

# THE PARSNIP

The next time you are sweating in your kitchen stirring up a cauldron of chicken soup save some of those parsnips you have sitting on top of the kitchen counter. Instead of throwing them into the bubbling brew, why not plant them? You may as well do it, you know, at least to satisfy your curiosity, for wouldn't you like to see how this project turns out? The results are quite pleasing.

The parsnip, like many other vegetables, is not new on the scene for it was raised as far back as Biblical times. Originally, though, it came from the Rhine Valley.

While civilization was busy cultivating itself, so was our friend, the parsnip, because finally, in 1592, it was produced in England. It didn't catch on in the United States, however, until the early 1800s when it was introduced and grown in New York for the first time.

The parsnip is a relative of the dill family and has a very deep root system. There aren't too many varieties available with the parsnip, only three. Sounding more like the names of swanky automobiles, they are Hollow Crown, Model, and All America. On second thought, they also sound like the names of fine racing horses, don't you think?

There are a few interesting facts that go hand in hand with the parsnip. For example, did you know that...

...the parsnip is rich in starches and sugars, thereby making it a very healthful food.

. . . it is fairly high in vitamins A and C and is a good energy booster.

. . . one pound of parsnip has 380 calories?

But that isn't all, for the parsnip makes a pretty house plant. To begin, choose one that is in good shape, one that is not wilting in the store. If there are any greens attached, snip them off so fresh new greenery can be grown.

With a vegetable brush, scrub the parsnip thoroughly under warm running water and dry it with some paper toweling. By washing it, the parsnip will become more susceptible for sprouting.

To continue, cut off a piece of the parsnip and place it cut side down into a container that has been filled with an all-purpose potting mixture. Leave about an inch of the parsnip exposed above the surface.

Remember, the parsnip has a deep root system. Because of this, make sure the pot you have selected has enough depth in which to accommodate this plant, for it is going to grow quickly.

Water lightly and place in a bright area. Germination occurs almost immediately. As growth progresses, pretty finely lobed leaves will appear. Later, a spike-like flower.

When the plant is actively growing, maintain a regular watering routine always keeping the soil moist, not too dry and never soggy. Feed about every two weeks with any of the available plant foods following the manufacturer's directions, but using only a quarter of the recommended dosage. Slowly build up to half, then full strength.

Keep in a south or west window, taking care to avoid a too hot sun. Otherwise the plant can wilt.

The parsnip plant is what is known as a biennial, that is, it will last for two years at a time. After that, it will begin to die back, which is in accordance with its nature.

# THE CUCUMBER

Last, but certainly not least, we continue with the cucumber. The cucumber is a vegetable that was once known as "coricumber." It's delicious when pickled and equally so when simply sliced into dieters' salads.

In fact, many an individual has succumbed to the cucumber's exquisite aroma while preparing it for mealtime and those scrumptious slices, nine times out of ten, never reached the dinner table.

You can grow cucumber seeds as an attractive hanging plant under the perfect sunny conditions of spring and summer. Warmth is very important here.

To begin, remove the seeds from a cucumber and rinse them under warm running water. Be careful not to let them get lost down the drain. Perhaps you have a closely meshed strainer you can use. Dry the seeds by rolling them gently in between paper toweling.

Select a four-inch container that has adequate drainage. Fill with an all-purpose potting mixture. Place seeds half-an-inch deep and cover with a thin layer of the soil. Water lightly.

Germination takes place in just a few days. Because the cucumber plant is such a fast grower, check the drainage holes for signs of transplanting. In time, you'll probably end up with a ten-inch pot.

Keep the plant in a south window because this is truly a sun-loving plant. Adopt a regular watering schedule, maintaining the soil at a constantly moist level. Never let it dry out.

Feed every two weeks with a water soluble fertilizer, carefully following the manufacturer's directions.

With growth progressing, such as it is, your cucumber plant is going to develop pretty, long, lobed leaves that will be about four inches in diameter. Tendrils develop, too. They make this plant a good candidate for a hanging planter.

As growth continues, attractive yellow bell-shaped flowers will appear. A point of interest lies in the fact that the male and the female both grow on the same vine. To pollinate, simply dab at each flower with a soft brush.

Don't be surprised, but later these flowers develop into cucumbers. However, according to the plant's natural growing pattern, after the cucumbers have been picked it will begin to die back.

The plant, all in all, should last approximately three months. Since it is so easy to grow, you shouldn't think twice about starting new seeds. Remember, they only take a few days in which to germinate.

# PART 5: GREENHOUSES

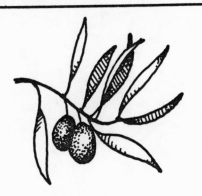

# HOW ABOUT
# A GREENHOUSE?

If you've ever considered building a greenhouse, there are a few decisions that must first be made. For example, how much money are you willing to spend and how much time are you going to be able to spend in it?

A hobby greenhouse can range from a simple polyethylene-covered framework that you can whip together in an afternoon for less than fifty dollars to a six thousand dollar fully automated conservatory.

By combining automatic controls, maintenance can be kept to an hour a week. Automatic controls are perfect for providing proper growing temperature, artificial light, watering, humidity, and ventilation.

You can save yourself a bundle of money if you have time to give and can skip the use of automatic controls. You can save even more if you can help in construction, but do so only if you are truly handy with tools. Even then, you'll still have to hire the services of a qualified plumber and electrician.

There are two basic types of greenhouses—attached and free standing. The attached lean-to is a greenhouse that is built against a building. This type of structure is limited to single or double-row plant benches with a total width of seven to twelve feet. It can be as long as the building it is attached to.

The advantage of the lean-to greenhouse is that it is usually close to available electricity, water and heat. However, this type of structure also has disadvantages, namely, limited space, limited light, and limited ventilation and temperature.

The attached even-span is a standard type of structure, one people usually visualize when they think about a greenhouse. It can accommodate two or three rows of plant benches. Although the cost of the even-span is greater than that of the lean-to type, it has wider flexibility in design and provides for more plants.

Because of its size and the greater amount of exposed glass area, the even-span greenhouse will cost more to heat.

The window-mounted greenhouse allows space in which to grow a few plants at relatively low cost for heating and cooling. This "reach-in" type of greenhouse is available in many standard sizes, either in single units or in tandem arrangements for large windows.

All you need are a few simple tools with which to remove the regular window from the frame and fasten the prefabricated window greenhouse in its place.

We now come to the freestanding greenhouse which is a separate structure unto itself. It consists of sidewalls, walls, and gable roof. Because it is unattached, this type of building can be made as small or as large as desired and can be built where it can receive the most sun.

A separate heating system is necessary unless the greenhouse is located close to a heated building. With this type of structure, more heat is required at night due to the additional glass.

Now that you have determined the kind of greenhouse you want, you must decide where you are going to put it.

Ideally, the best site for your greenhouse would be one that is well drained, nearly level, and has full exposure to sunlight. It would slope slightly to the south and have a windbreak on the side of the prevailing wind.

However, one can do only just so much with what one has, so in case the above-mentioned ideal location is not available, let's start from scratch. The first choice should be on the south or southeast side of the house in a sunny location.

The east side is the second best location for that's where it will capture the most November to February sunlight. The next best locations are the southwest and west. Northside is the least desirable of all locations.

When choosing a site for your greenhouse, you may place it in a partly shaded area during the summer when light reduction is not too drastic but beware of the possibility of falling limbs from trees that can break through the glass of the greenhouse.

Sometimes you can place a greenhouse against a door, window, or basement entrance. This lets you use heat from your house to grow plants, makes your greenhouse more accessible, and saves on construction costs. However, your home heating will show a marked increase.

If you have an L-shaped house, you can save on the cost of two greenhouse walls by building the greenhouse into the shape of the "L."

Whether your greenhouse runs north and south or east and west is not as important as wind protection.

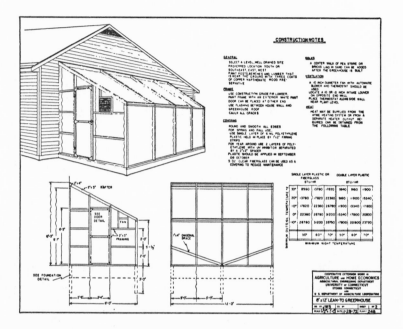

Protect your greenhouse from winds by locating it so existing buildings will shield it or by providing it with a windbreak hedge or fence.

Before you can start to build your greenhouse, dimensions and width must be determined. Width is the most important decision to make because once the greenhouse has been constructed no alterations can be made. Length, however, can always be increased if more space is desired.

Determine the width of your greenhouse by adding the widths of the plant benches and the walks. Allow approximately six inches for walls at either side and two inches for air circulation space between the sidewalls and the benches.

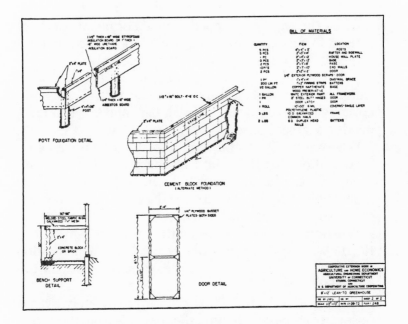

Side benches should be no wider than two to three feet across. Center benches, six feet across. They should be placed no wider than to permit you to work comfortably. Determine the width of the walks by how they are to be used. If the walks are to be used only as a place in which to stand while working on your plants, an eighteen or a nineteen inch walk is sufficiently wide. However, if you plan to bring a wheelbarrow into the greenhouse, walks, naturally, should be wider, about twenty-four to thirty inches across.

Determine the length of your greenhouse by multiplying the number of plants you can grow across the benches. Then round off the measurement so that no glass will need to be cut to fill odd sash bar spacings. A sash, by the way, is a shaped wooden or metal bar that is used in the construction of a sash or frame and designed to hold and support the glass securely to it.

Standard glass sizes are sixteen by twenty-four, eighteen by twenty, and twenty by twenty inches. Larger glass sizes mean few sash bars and less shadow inside the greenhouse.

When you figure the length of your glass greenhouse, allow for the width of the projecting part of each sash bar plus a fraction of an inch clearance.

The height of the greenhouse depends upon the desired height of the eave. An eave height of five feet is satisfactory for side benches with low-growing plants. If you want to grow tall plants, such as the avocado and papaya, for example, the eave should be six to seven feet high.

The pitch of the roof should be approximately twenty-seven degrees. Its height, the distance from the sidewall to the center of the greenhouse, and the roof pitch determine the height of the center of the greenhouse.

For example, in an even-span greenhouse that is eighteen feet wide, the distance from the sidewall to the center of the greenhouse is nine feet. The difference in height between the center of the greenhouse and the eave will be four-and-a-half feet. If the eave is five feet high, the greenhouse should be nine-and-a-half feet at the center.

Whether you build a glass, fiberglass, or plastic greenhouse, it will pay you to shop around for ideas. Greenhouses have supporting frameworks made of wood, aluminum, iron, or galvanized pipe. Some have curved eaves while others have flat ones. Some are glass or plastic from the ground up. All types have advantages and disadvantages. And by the way, most local governments require a building permit to erect a greenhouse.

Glass is the traditional greenhouse covering. It is available in many designs to blend with almost any type of architecture. These structures may have slanted sides, straight sides and eaves, or curved eaves.

Aluminum, maintenance-free glass construction has very attractive lines and provides a large growing area. It also assures you of a weathertight structure which minimizes heat costs and retains humidity.

Small prefabricated glass greenhouses are available for a "do-it-yourself" installation. These come in a variety of models and can fit almost any space and pocketbook.

The disadvantages of glass are that it is easily broken, it is expensive, and requires a much better type of construction than fiberglass and plastic.

Fiberglass is lightweight, strong, and practically hailproof. Corrugated panels eight to twelve feet long and flat fiberglass in rolls are available in twenty-four to forty-eight inch widths. Thicknesses range from 3/-64 to 3/32 of an inch.

Poor grades of fiberglass discolors and the discoloring reduces light penetration. On the other hand, if you use a better grade of this material, you may make your fiberglass greenhouse as expensive as a glass one. In selecting fiberglass, select the clearest grade. Never use colored fiberglass.

Plastic greenhouses are increasing in popularity for many reasons. For one thing, construction cost per square foot is generally one-sixth to one-tenth the cost of glass greenhouses. Also, plastic greenhouses can be heated as satisfactorily as glass ones.

Furthermore, plants growing under plastic have the same quality as those that are grown under glass. And, plastic greenhouses are considered temporary structures and usually carry a low assessment rate for tax purposes. In fact, they might not be taxed at all.

Plastic greenhouses can be made of polyethylene (PE), polyvinyl chloride (PVC), copolymers of these materials, and other readily available clear materials. Polyethlene must be replaced each year because it deteriorates rapidly in strong summer sunlight.

Other materials such as PVC or copolymers with ultraviolet (UV) inhibitors last longer. With polyethylene, the advantages lie in the fact that they are low in cost and are lightweight. Polyethylene also stands up well in fall, winter, and spring weather and lets plenty of light through for good plant growth. However, polyethylene constantly exposed to the sun deteriorates drastically and must be replaced each year. Ultraviolet light energy causes polyethylene to break down. This first deterioration occurs along the rafters.

Ultraviolet-inhibited polyethylene lasts longer than regular ployethylene and has an inhibitor that prevents the rapid breakdown caused by ultraviolet light. UV-inhibited polyethylene is available in two and six-mill thicknesses up to forty feet wide and one hundred feet long.

Also, polyethylene permits the passage of much of the reradiated heat energy given off by the soil and plants inside the greenhouse. Therefore, a polyethylene greenhouse loses heat more quickly than a glass greenhouse both during sunny periods and after sunset. This is an advantage during the day, but a disadvantage at night.

In polyvinyl chloride, that is PVC or vinyl, vinyls from three to twelve mils thick are available for greenhouse coverings. These materials are soft and pliable. Some are transparent while others are transluscent. They are usually available in four to six foot widths. Larger widths can be made by electronically sealing several smaller widths together.

Vinyls cost two to five times as much as polyethylene. When carefully installed, eight or twelve mil vinyl holds up for as long as five years. Be aware that vinyl attracts dust and dirt from the air and has to be washed every once in awhile.

There are different types of frames connected with greenhouses. In building an A-frame structure, consideration must be given to the placement of cross rafters. They should be placed at least one-third of the distance down from the ridge on the outer rafters. Otherwise, it will be difficult to work around the cross rafters in applying an insulating layer of plastic.

When cross-rafter support is high in the peak of the greenhouse, an essentially clear-span type of structure permits easy application of an inner layer of plastic. The inner layer can be applied under the cross rafter supports, leaving a small triangular airspace in the peak of the house.

Diagonal bracing wires provide added strength to an A-frame structure. This type of greenhouse is among the least difficult to build.

Rigid-frame structures have been designed in widths up to forty feet. Here, there are no columns to hold up the roof section. The best available rigid-frame greenhouse has six foot sidewalls and is designed for thirty, thirty-six, or forty foot widths.

A prefabricated greenhouse built with curved laminated wood rafters is commercially available. It has low headroom and the structure has to be raised high on the foundation sidewalls in order to grow tall plants.

Panel-frame greenhouses are a modification of the sashhouse, which is a small plastic greenhouse used for growing plants for later transplanting. This structure requires accurate carpentry and construction costs are higher than other frames due to added lumber and labor needed to build the panels.

Advantages of panels are that they can be quickly installed and taken down and stored during the summer. This increases the life of the plastic panels. Panel greenhouses can be easily ventilated, too.

Quonset greenhouses have the same general shape as the Quonset huts of World War II. Some have been constructed of wood, but usually the frames are metal. The half-circle frames are covered with one piece of wide plastic. These houses are normally up to twenty feet wide.

The advantage here is the ease of construction and covering. Ventilation is accomplished by the use of exhaust fans at the ends of the houses.

A pipe frame structure can be used to frame an air-inflated greenhouse. Air is introduced into a chamber formed by two layers of four or six mil film.

The effect of the air under slight pressure is to force the inner layer of film over the circular greenhouse pipe frames. The outer layer assumes a circular shape over the frame and rides on a cushion of air. The outer layer lifts three to four inches from the frame at the top and one to two inches from the frame at the foundation. Air enters the chamber through six-inch plastic tubing. A manometer is used to measure static air pressure between the two layers of film.

You can heat your greenhouse efficiently with coal, electricity, gas and oil. Heating equipment can be a space heater, a forced-air heater, a hot-water or steam system, or electric heater. Radiant heat lamps over plants and soil heating cables under plants can also be used.

Ventilation is also important because even during cold weather a greenhouse can get too warm on a bright, sunny day. If you use hand-operated roof vents, they'll require frequent temperature checks. As outdoor weather changes, sashes must be opened and closed by hand to prevent plants from getting too hot or cold.

Automatic ventilation eliminates manual work and is the best way to cool a greenhouse, but fan and duct ventilation may also be used. Plastic ducts are suspended by wires from the roof of the greenhouse. The fan-heater-louver unit gives positive air flow and the polyethylene duct distributes the incoming air evenly throughout the structure.

When protection from the sun is needed, use rollup screens of wood or aluminum, vinyl plastic shading, or paint-on materials. Then, the use of an evaporative cooler or fan and pad system eliminates excessive heat and adds beneficial humidity to the greenhouse atmosphere. With an evaporative cooler, moist cool air is circulated throughout the entire greenhouse.

Mist sprays are used in propagating to keep the atmosphere humid. The most popular method is by means of time clocks but another method can be used where the system controls the cycles by evaporation from a mechanical or electronic leaf or screen.

Carbon dioxide and light are, of course, needed for plant growth. Greenhouses often have too little carbon dioxide during the day to effectively utilize available light so that by enriching the atmosphere with $CO_2$, plant growth can be accelerated. Inexpensive metric kits are available for determining the $CO_2$ level in your greenhouse.

You can get $CO_2$ in a number of ways. Bottled, for one, which has been liquified from a burning process. It is kept under pressure and is controlled by means of a metering device.

Dry ice may be placed in the greenhouse in a pressure bottle and stored until it is needed. Burned sulfurfree gaseous fuels such as natural gas, L P gas, or a liquid carbon fuel such as kerosene is also available.

You will also need artificial lighting and control units in your greenhouse. Artificial light can be used to provide high intensity light when increased plant growth is desired. It can also be used to extend the hours of natural daylight or to provide a night interruption to maintain the plants on long-day conditions. Inexpensive light meters are available for measuring the light intensity in greenhouses; the most common measure is foot-candles.

As a gardener you will be concerned with the air temperature required inside the greenhouse and the minimum outside temperature that your heating equipment must overcome.

Space heaters can maintain a minium of sixty degrees inside the greenhouse while higher temperatures on the plant benches can be provided with soil-warming equipment.

Automatic controls are also important. Without them, switching lights, fans, pumps, heaters, and misters on and off at a prescribed time would be a complicated and laborious chore. Many time clocks, photocells, thermostats, and other controls are commercially available. When used individually or in combination they provide complete and convenient control.

The plan you see in this book is for an eight-by-twelve attached greenhouse, diagram # 248. You can get it for a slight fee by writing to the Northeast Regional Agricultural Engineering Service. For two dollars they will also send you their manual called Hobby Greenhouses and Other Structures. In writing, direct your letter to the following address:

Robert Parson, Manager
NRAES-2
Riley-Robb Hall
Cornell University
Ithaca, New York 14853

For $1.25 you may also write away for plans at this address:

Northwestern Vocational Curriculum
   Management Center
Commission for Vocational Education,
Building 17
Airdustrial Park
Olympia, Washington 98504

In addition, plans and drawings for plastic green-houses and propagating frames are available free from your State agricultural experiment station, county agricultural agent, extension agricultural agent, extension agricultural engineer at your State university, or are for sale by the Superintendent of Documents, U.S. Government Printing Office, Washington, D.C. 20402.

If you do not know the location of your State university, send your request to Agricultural Engineer, Extension Service, U.S. Department of Agriculture, Washington, D.C 20250. He will forward your request to the correct university.

So—what do you think? How about a greenhouse?

# PART 6: GLOSSARY

# GLOSSARY

**Aeration**  Free movement of air around roots of plants. Prevented in waterlogged or compacted soil.

**Annuals**  Plants that live one year or less. During this time, when the plant is actively growing, flowers produce seeds after which the plant dies. Example: beans, peas, squash.

**Chelated**  Molecular form in which certain nutrients, such as iron, are easily absorbed by the plant.

**Chlorophyll**  The green coloring matter maintained in plants' cells.

**Compost**  Decayed matter such as leaves, manure, sludge, which is mixed with soil and fertilizer to enrich the soil.

**Cotyledons**  Leaves which contain stored food for initial seedling growth.

**Crown**  Growing point above the root where the top of the plant develops, such as with carrots and pineapples.

**Damping off**  A disease which causes seedlings to die soon after they germinate, either before or after emerging from the soil.

(183

**Fungicide** A pesticide chemical used to control plant diseases caused by fungi.

**Germination** The sprouting of a seed and the beginning of new plant growth.

**Growing medium** Soil or soil substitute prepared by combining such materials as peat, vermiculite or sand. These are used for growing potted plants or germinating seed.

**Hill** Raising the soil in a slight mound for planting.

**Humus** Decomposed organic matter with which to improve the texture of soil.

**Inorganic** In fertilizers, those produced chemically. An occurence not arising from natural growth.

**Insecticide** Chemicals used to control insects either on contact or as a stomach poison.

**K** Symbol for potash.

**Leaf mold** Partially decayed leaves used for improving soil structure.

**Leggy and scraggly** Weak-stemmed and spindly plants with sparse foliage. This is caused by too much heat, too much shade, overcrossing, and overfertilization.

**Legumes** Plants that take nitrogen from the air with

certain bacteria that live on its roots. Examples: peas and beans.

**Light soil**  Soil that is easy to cultivate, retains little moisture and has a coarse or sandy texture.

**Loam**  Soil consisting of less than 52% sand, 28% to 50% silt, and 7% to 27% clay. This makes an ideal soil texture for gardening.

**Micro-organism**  Any microscopic animal or plant that may cause a plant disease or have the beneficial effect of decomposing plant residue to become humus.

**Mites**  Extremely small sucking insects that infect plants.

**Nitrogen**  Essential plant nutrient for growth and green color. Available in organic and inorganic forms.

**NPK**  Symbols for three primary nutrients needed by plants. N is for nitrogen, P for phosphate, and K is for potash or potassium. The percentages of these elements is always listed on a package of fertilizer and is listed in this order.

**Organic matter**  Portion of soil resulting from decomposition of plant material. This helps to maintain good soil structure.

**P**  Symbol for phosphate.

**Pan**   A flat or shallow pan used for germinating seeds.

**Peat moss**   Partially decomposed plant life taken from bogs used as a rooting medium and for soil conditioning.

**Perennials**   Plants that normally live more than two years.

**Pesticide**   Chemical control of pests.

**Pesticide residue**   Material that remains on a plant after the application of a pesticide.

**pH**   The chemical symbol used to give the reading of acidity in the soil. Scales range from 0 to 14, with 7 the neutral reading. Readings of less than 7 show acid soil. Readings above that show an alkaline condition in the soil.

**Phosphate**   One of the three major plant nutrients.

**Pinching**   Removing growth to stimulate branching.

**Plant nutrient**   An ingredient furnishing nourishment to promote growth in plants. Examples: nitrogen, phosphorous, potassium, iron and sulfur, which is supplied by the soil, organic matter and fertilizers.

**Potash**   One of the three major plant nutrients essential for plant growth. Same as potassium.

**Pot bound**   Plants whose roots completely fill a container and surround the soil ball in which they are growing. This restricts normal top growth of the plant.

**Potting mixture**  Combination of soil and other ingredients such as peat, sand, or vermiculite; used for starting seed or growing plants in containers.

**Pruning**  Removing branches to control the size and shape of a plant. It controls fruiting and strengthens and improves the appearance of a plant. Removing dead or broken branches.

**Rest period**  Normal period of inactivity in growth of a plant. Dormancy.

**Scale**  Tiny sucking insects that leave cottony masses on foliage.

**Seedling**  Young plant developing from a germinating seed. The first true leaves are usually already developed.

**Sphagnum**  Mosses which grow in bogs. When decomposed this becomes peat moss.

**Sucker**  A stem that rises from a root. It should be removed because it will weaken the plant.

**Systemic**  Pesticide matter absorbed by plants to make them toxic to feeding insects.

**Tamping**   Lightly firming soil over seeds or newly transplanted plants.

**Tendril**   Slender twining organ found along stems of certain plants. This helps the vine to climb and cling to a support such as a trellis. Example: grape.

**Thinning**   Removing young plants to provide more space in which remaining plants can grow.

**Trace elements**   Minerals such as boron, manganese, iron and zinc. So-named because only a trace or small amount of these elements are needed by plants.

**Transplanting**   Digging up a plant and moving it to another location.

**Trellis**   An open lattice structure used to support plants.

**Tuber**   Thickened underground branch with many buds or eyes. Thickening occurs because of the accumulation of reserved food. Example: potato.

**Vermiculite**   Soft substance added to soil to help it retain moisture.

**Viable**   A seed that is alive and capable of germinating.

**Wettable powders**   Pesticide blended with a filler and wetting agent so that it can be mixed with water.

**Wilting**   Drooping of leaves and stems due to under-watering. Can also result from root damage, disease, injury, or hot drying winds.